"It's easy to think cyberbullying is out of everyone's cor
show teens how they can use their power and influence
of cruelty and replace it with a culture of kindness. Thes
everything there is to know about cyberbullying, and the
realistic and smart. Read this book!"

—**Rachel Simmons,** author of the *New York Times* best seller *Odd Girl Out:
The Hidden Culture of Aggression in Girls*

"There couldn't be a more effective book when it comes to understanding,
identifying, and combating bullying in any form."

—**Kevin Curwick,** creator of @OsseoNiceThings and founder of the "Nice It
Forward" movement

"*Words Wound* is the first book that has been specifically written for teens
to help them confront cyberbullying. Whether they are being targeted, see
cyberbullying happening to others, or want to promote kindness within their
schools, this book provides practical and proven advice."

—**Dr. Michele Borba,** bullying expert and author of 22 books including *Building
Moral Intelligence*

"This powerful resource teaches students effective social networking skills
and provides educators with insights to help teens manage their online
reputations and lives."

—**Patrick Mott,** teen social media expert

"*Words Wound* is the most important book you can purchase today!"

—**Sue Scheff,** author of *Google Bomb* and *Wit's End*

Words Wound

Wound

Delete Cyberbullying and Make Kindness Go Viral

Justin W. Patchin and Sameer Hinduja

free spirit
PUBLISHING®

ary of Congress Cataloging-in-Publication Data
chin, Justin W., 1977–
Words wound : delete cyberbullying and make kindness go viral / by Justin W. Patchin, Ph.D., and Sameer
Hinduja, Ph.D.
     pages cm
   Includes index.
   Summary: "Two expert researchers on bullying prevention speak directly to teens about how they can end
cyberbullying. It provides them with numerous peer anecdotes and strategies they can use to help create
kinder schools and communities"— Provided by publisher.
   Audience: Age 13 plus.
   ISBN-13: 978-1-57542-451-4 (pbk.)
   ISBN-10: 1-57542-451-7 (pbk.)
1. Cyberbullying—Prevention—Juvenile literature. 2. Bullying—Prevention—Juvenile literature. 3.
   Computer crimes—Juvenile literature. 4. Internet and teenagers—Juvenile literature. I. Hinduja,
   Sameer, 1978- II. Title.
   HV6773.15.C92P38 2013
   302.34'302854678—dc23   2013035968

eBook ISBN: 978-1-57542-602-0

Reading Level High School–Adult; Interest Level Ages 13 & up;
Fountas & Pinnell Guided Reading Level Z+

Edited by Alison Behnke
Cover and interior design by Tasha Kenyon

10 9 8 7 6 5 4 3 2 1
Printed in the United States of America
B10951013

Free Spirit Publishing Inc.
Minneapolis, MN
(612) 338-2068
help4kids@freespirit.com
www.freespirit.com

Free Spirit offers competitive pricing.
Contact edsales@freespirit.com for pricing information on
multiple quantity purchases.

This book is dedicated to teens—to the ones who shared their stories with us for this book and the ones whose stories have yet to be told. We believe in your abilities to make the world a better, kinder place, and we hope *Words Wound* helps you in this pursuit.

—Justin and Sameer

Contents

Status Updates—Activities for You to Do

You may download these pages at **www.freespirit.com/wordswoundactivities**. Use the password **deletebullying**.

Introduction

When I was in 10th grade, I was cyberbullied. Girls would send me threats in texts and leave me voicemails saying, "I'm going to run you over with my truck," and "you might as well die, nobody likes you." They would also post on my Facebook wall saying things like "you're ugly," and "nobody likes you, move away nasty anorexic psycho."

I didn't know how to handle these posts, texts, and voicemails. I was so scared to go to school every day, because I knew that the girls would do something to me. And it was not only one girl—it was a big group of girls. They would follow me around the school and say things to me, and I tried to ignore it the best I could, but at times it got so hard to do that. I would sometimes not even go to lunch, because I felt like I had no friends.

I would go home and cry to my mom. She didn't understand what was going on until I finally decided to tell her. She went to the principal. She told him, "My daughter will not be going back to school anymore because of the bullying." They said I had to. Then my mom took me to a doctor, who wrote the school a letter saying, "Maria is mentally and emotionally too unstable to attend school." My mom convinced the principal to let me go to school for a few hours after the normal day ended so I could do my homework without students terrorizing me each and every day.

Bullying is a horrible thing. Nobody really knows what it's like until they are put through it themselves.

Please, never bully someone.

—Maria, 17, Wisconsin

We hear stories like Maria's all the time. *All the time.* And behind all of these stories are teens who just want to be left alone to make their way through school, to pursue their interests, and to have people care about them. Really, that's all that most of us want out of life: To have friends and family who are always there for us, who love and support us—and to be treated with basic respect by everyone else. Even if you have these things, though, sometimes life isn't easy. Things don't always work out the way you want them to or hope they will. It can get really rough sometimes as you deal with all your day-to-day stresses and responsibilities: homework and tests, extracurricular activities, relationship troubles, disagreements at home, arguments with friends, and—on top of all that—trying to figure out who you are and who you want to be.

You can't ignore or avoid these challenges. But you *can* try to prevent other problems that affect many teens, and bullying is one of them. Despite what some people might say, bullying is not a "rite of passage." It is not something that "everyone just has to deal with." It's *never* okay to be bullied or to bully others. Never. And physical bullying isn't the only painful type of harassment. Of course, pushing, shoving, punching, tripping, and all other physical forms of bullying are wrong, and everyone knows it (even though these things still happen). But just because cyberbullying does not leave visible marks doesn't mean it should be dismissed. *Words wound.* And the pain that words can cause often pierces much deeper than the pain of physical bullying. Naima, a 14-year-old from New York, told us, *"They say sticks and stones may break my bones but names will never hurt me. That quote is a lie and I don't believe it. Sticks and stones may cause nasty cuts, but those cuts and scars will heal. Insulting words hurt and sometimes take forever to heal."*

Defining the Problem

Cyberbullying is harassment and intimidation that takes place through text messages, online posts, email, or other electronic forms of communication. You might feel like there isn't much of a difference between your online life and your offline life. But cyberbullying is a specific form of bullying, with its own unique problems and challenges. And whether bullying happens at school or online, through rumors spread on bathroom walls or Facebook walls, it's not cool.

Why We Wrote This Book

When we hear stories from teens who have been cyberbullied, it makes us sad—and it also makes us mad. We're sad because someone has been hurt by the carelessness and cruelty of others. And we get mad because it *still* happens so often. We do not accept the idea about bullying that says it's always going to exist because it always has. Personally, we think that defense is a cop-out. And our view isn't based on the idealistic hope that one day everyone will hold hands and sing folk songs together.

Instead, it's based on the fact that we know what a school without bullying looks like. It's not a make-believe place that only exists on a cheesy TV show. We've been in many schools across the United States that reject any sort of bullying. It's a great feeling to walk through the halls of these schools. They are safe, welcoming, and fun places for students and teachers to be—places of respect, kindness, and a mindset that focuses on "us" instead of "me."

For example, North Stafford High School in Stafford, Virginia, has worked hard to build supportive and positive attitudes at school, and to develop ways for this idea to take root throughout the student body. Treating others the way you'd like to be treated is simply part of being a North Stafford Wolverine. Another school with a climate of kindness is Lake Brantley High School in Altamonte Springs, Florida. It's home to a movement called "To Be Kind" (TBK), which challenges and encourages everyone on campus to consciously choose mindsets and actions that build others up rather than tear them down. TBK caught on quickly at Lake Brantley, and it has even been adopted by other schools in Florida and beyond.

These examples prove something that we've discovered through many years of working on the problems of bullying and cyberbullying. We've learned that people, schools, and communities can take specific steps to prevent, reduce, and respond to all forms of harassment. We wanted to take this knowledge and turn it into a book for *you*. After all, when cyberbullying happens at your school or between your friends, you deal with the stress, anger, and hurt feelings that result. And you can lead the way to stopping this cycle. We're not saying that adults can't be any help. But the truth is that real, lasting change starts with you.

Think of all of the teens who do amazing things in their neighborhoods, cities, states, and countries. You've heard about them on the news. You've watched videos about them on YouTube. Maybe you've seen them in your own community. Each of their efforts started with a simple idea and one small step. If you care about deleting cyberbullying and making kindness go viral, take that first small step. See where it takes you. This book will help you along the way.

For many, the idea of kids and technology may conjure up images of cyberbullying and sexting. I started the @westhighbros Twitter account to end cyberbullying at my school and to make it a better place to be in general. Our account proves that people my age really do great things with technology. The @westhighbros account (and its Facebook version) is used for writing compliments—we call them "comps." We write comps mainly to our classmates at Iowa City West High, but we've also written to the principal of our cross-town rival, to celebrities, and even to President Obama. Most of the time people respond with a thank you. This is our method for combating bullying and negativity.

Bullying remains a very serious problem. Even more frightening, we regularly hear news reports about bullying being a factor in teen suicide. While it may be impossible to eliminate bullying completely, my goal is to impact one person at a time. You might be thinking this idea is dumb, but ever since we started our Twitter and Facebook pages, bullying has decreased by over 60 percent at our school. I encourage anyone reading this to think of ways they can help spread their own comps. It could change your whole community—it certainly changed mine.

—Jeremiah Anthony, 17, Iowa

Why Us?

You might be asking yourself, "What do these guys know about cyberbullying?" It's a fair question.

One thing we know is how it feels to be bullied. Both of us went through it when we were in school. It was awful. We remember our experiences vividly, and they had a big impact on our lives. So while cyberbullying may not have been a big problem yet when we were teens, we *do* understand the problem of bullying from a personal point of view. That understanding is what makes us want to work even harder at ending the hate and harassment we've seen and heard about.

Plus, we've talked with thousands of teens (and adults) at schools, libraries, and youth centers around the United States and in other countries about their experiences with bullying and cyberbullying. We've presented to students in big groups, and we've worked with them one-on-one. We have also talked to parents, including some who have lost children to suicide that resulted in part from cyberbullying experiences. The personal stories we've heard—from the hopeful to the heartbreaking—motivate and inspire us to keep working toward positive change.

As part of this work, we also run the Cyberbullying Research Center (**cyberbullying.us**). We use the center to share information about cyberbullying. Lots of people visit our website every day. Many share with us their own experiences with cyberbullying. In return, we do whatever we can to help.

Through all of these efforts, we've learned what works and what doesn't when it comes to deleting cyberbullying. We share those lessons with you in this book. We've also made a website specifically for you at **wordswound.org**. It's a place where we can keep the conversation going with you about your questions, worries, ideas, thoughts, strategies, and successes.

How to Use This Book

In *Words Wound,* you'll find tons of ideas for preventing, reducing, and combating cyberbullying. Some of them are for people who are being bullied. Some are for people who might have bullied others, or for those who have witnessed bullying and want to do more to stop it. Others focus on how you can make your school a kinder place. Of course, not every single idea will work in every case. So you should feel free to use these suggestions as starting points and modify them to fit your situation.

Exactly how you read this book is up to you. You can read it from beginning to end, or you can jump to the chapter that interests you at the moment. We want it be a toolkit for you. We hope you'll pick it up often, and use it whenever you need to help yourself and others who might be dealing with online harassment, mistreatment, or other problems.

The book is divided into three parts. **Part One** gives you the facts about cyberbullying and tips on what to do if it's affecting you. In **Part Two**, you'll explore ways to be kind and respectful, help others cope with bullying, and stay safe online. **Part Three** talks about what you can do to make your school and community kinder places where bullying isn't allowed.

Here's more on what you'll find in each chapter:

<u>**Chapter 1**</u> gives you an overview of what cyberbullying is, who does it, and who it affects.

<u>**Chapter 2**</u> lays out what you need to know if you're being bullied, and gives you lots of ideas for how you can respond. One big thing that we want you to remember from this chapter is that no one deserves to be disrespected or treated badly—ever.

<u>**Chapter 3**</u> looks at the other side of the equation: the bullying itself. It gives you guidance if you've ever cyberbullied or harassed someone else online, or if you've thought about doing so. It also explains the potential consequences of cyberbullying—in your social group, school, and community, and even from the police.

In **Chapter 4,** you'll find out what you can do when you see cyberbullying happening to someone else, and how you can speak up rather than stand by.

Chapter 5 describes smart ways to act online to protect yourself from cyberbullying and other online risks. There are plenty of simple things you can do (and some you should *not* do!) to safeguard your identity, personal information, and experiences in cyberspace to reduce the chances that you will be the target of a cyberbully. The ideas may not protect you 100 percent (unfortunately, nothing will), but they *will* help.

In **Chapters 6 and 7,** we offer suggestions for taking action to make your school or community cyberbully-free. And it doesn't stop there. You can do much more than *just* stop bullying and cyberbullying. You can help make your school a place where kindness and respect replace cruelty and meanness. Imagine a school where students are allowed to just be themselves, without having to deal with hate, rejection, jealousy, and drama. When that happens, everyone is so much more able to focus on school, friendships, relationships, and the future.

Throughout the book, you'll also find a variety of other features. You'll see stories from teens, telling about their experiences with cyberbullying. You'll find quotes from famous people talking about bullying, standing up for yourself, and more. You'll also see pieces called "Think About It." These pose questions for you to mull over yourself or discuss with friends. And at the end of each chapter, you'll find a "Status Update." These are activities to help you (and others) think more about cyberbullying and your own experiences. You can also find these Status Updates online. See the table of contents for more information on how to download the activity pages.

About the Stories

All of the stories that you will read in this book are true. They come from teens who have been cyberbullied, have cyberbullied others, or are working to end cyberbullying and create kindness. In some cases we include the person's real name—especially if he or she has taken a stand against cyberbullying, such as Kylie LeMay in Chapter 4, or Kevin Curwick in Chapter 7. But most of the time, to protect people's privacy, we've changed their names. And while we have edited the stories to make them clearer, we've never changed their meaning. As we wrote this book, we also worked closely with teens to make sure the book would be useful to you and true to your experiences.

Beyond the Pages

Maybe you're reading this book because you're dealing with a rough cyberbullying situation yourself, or maybe it's because you want to help a friend who is struggling with being harassed online. Maybe you feel like there's too much drama, negativity, and cruelty at your school, and you want to do something about the cyberbullying you see around you. Or maybe a teacher has assigned this book for a class. Whatever the reason, make sure you stay in the know on the who, what, when, where, and why of cyberbullying. Visit our website at wordswound.org and take a look at the fact sheets, resources, and activities we've posted there. Talk with your friends about what they're seeing and experiencing online. You can also chat with teachers, your school counselor, or other adults at your school (and beyond) to learn more about what kind of cyberbullying situations they've seen or heard about. These different points of view will help you wrap your head around the big-picture problem of cyberbullying—which will help you figure out the best way to fight it.

We Want to Hear from You

We hope that *Words Wound* inspires you to help change the way you, your friends, and your classmates think about and act toward each other. Go at it by yourself, or tackle it with help from friends, teachers, parents, and others. It won't be easy, and it won't happen overnight, but the challenge will be worth it.

Finally, keep us in the loop! You can reach us at our website and on social media. You can also email us at **help@wordswound.org**. We're ready to hear what you have to say, and we'll do what we can to help you along the way. We also want to know the details of your successes. We're eager to hear from you, and we look forward to helping you make a difference in your school, community, and life.

—Justin and Sameer

Part One

Cyberbullying—What You Need to Know

Chapter 1

The Scoop on Cyberbullying

I've been bullied my whole life and made fun of endlessly. In 8th grade people called me fat, worthless, ugly, piece of sh*t, slut, *and so on. Every day I would hear these things for hours and would go home wanting to kill myself. Then I'd go online and see it all over again. It never went away. I developed an eating disorder and attempted suicide. In high school the bullying got even worse. By the end of my sophomore year I only weighed 100 pounds, I was self-harming, and I had attempted suicide 18 times. Words can hurt. They can kill. And typed words hurt most of all because they're ALWAYS going to be there. No one should go through this. Please speak up. One day we can finally end this injustice together.*

—Sasha, 16, Michigan

What Is Cyberbullying?

If you ask around about cyberbullying, you might find that many people have different ideas of what it actually is. In this book and in our research, we define cyberbullying as a situation in which someone intentionally and repeatedly harasses, makes fun of, or mistreats another person on social media sites, through text messages,

"I was called really horrible, profane names ... there was a certain point in my high school years where I just couldn't even focus on class because I was so embarrassed all the time. I was so ashamed of who I was."
—*Lady Gaga*

13

or in other ways online. This definition contains four important elements that make bullying different from teasing or arguing, for example. It also helps distinguish between in-person bullying and cyberbullying. Cyberbullying is:

Intentional. Cyberbullying doesn't happen by accident. It's made up of behaviors that are deliberate and willful.

Harmful. Cyberbullying causes someone else humiliation, pain, or fear.

Repeated. Generally speaking, a single hurtful email or one mean comment on an Instagram picture isn't cyberbullying. When the harassment happens many times over an extended period, or involves a lot of other people joining in as an image or post goes viral, it becomes bullying.

Online and/or electronic. Cyberbullying happens using computers, cell phones, and other electronic devices.

Maybe you've heard people call some of this online behavior "digital drama." Cyberbullying is a *type* of digital drama, but it happens on a much more serious and abusive level, and it happens over and over again. It's important to keep in mind that not everything unpleasant that happens online equals cyberbullying. For example, just about all of us have received spam and other unwanted emails, which is sometimes annoying or even troubling. Most of us have gotten into a disagreement with someone else online, whether a stranger or a close friend. And it's not especially uncommon to send or receive an angry text or IM at one time or another. But none of this is cyberbullying. If you have an argument on Facebook with a friend, or if your boyfriend or girlfriend breaks up with you via text and says something mean about you on Twitter, that hurts. But remember, cyberbullying is when those kinds of

Forms of Cyberbullying

Cyberbullying can—and does—happen anywhere online, using anything that can connect to the Internet, from a cell phone to a tablet to a gaming console. Most cyberbullying happens on popular websites such as Twitter, Tumblr, Facebook, Instagram, and YouTube. Following are some of the most common forms of cyberbullying. Have you experienced any of these things, or do you know someone who has?

- Posting mean or hurtful comments online
- Posting a picture or video online that is embarrassing, disrespectful, or cruel
- Creating a Web page intended to hurt or embarrass someone else
- Spreading rumors through email, text messages, IM, social media, or other electronic communications
- Threatening someone online or through text messages
- Pretending to be someone else online and acting in a way that is embarrassing or painful for the person
- Using online gaming devices to be hateful, threatening, or abusive

actions happen again and again over weeks or months—especially when the person doing them is told to stop or knows that what they are doing is really bothering you.

Bullying's repetitive nature is a big part of what makes it so painful. After all, if someone you know makes fun of you online every single day, that's going to be on your mind an awful lot. In class, between classes, before school, after school, on the weekends—you're going to be worried about seeing that person in real life, and you'll probably be trying to think of ways to avoid him or her. This worry and distraction is going to make it harder for you to learn and study, enjoy your friendships and your family, and focus on sports, clubs, and other activities.

All types of bullying can have this negative effect on a person's life and happiness. But as bullying has moved online, and as many of us get used

CYBERBULLYING CAN AFFECT YOU 24/7.

to checking phones, tablets, and laptops almost constantly, it can really feel like there's no escape. Cyberbullying can affect you 24/7.

How Common Is Cyberbullying?

If you pay attention to news reports of cyberbullying—or if you know people who talk about the topic a lot—you might think that cyberbullying is an epidemic, happening everywhere all the time. When we first started studying this subject over a decade ago, we would print out any news article we saw that talked about cyberbullying—because it happened pretty rarely (or at least it was reported rarely). Now, it seems, cyberbullying is in the news almost every day.

Cyberbullying definitely is a problem. Like any other form of bullying or harassment, it's not okay if it affects even one person and makes his or her life painful, difficult, or lonely. But is it really as common as the news reports suggest? This is one of the questions we've tried to answer with our research.

What we've learned is that most teens are *not* directly involved in cyberbullying. But we've also found that cyberbullying does seem to be increasing. Here's some of the information we've gathered:

- Over the past 10 years, an average of about 24 percent of the students we surveyed told us that they had been the target of cyberbullying at some point. About 11 percent of them had experienced it in the previous 30 days.

- Roughly 17 percent of students admitted to us that they had cyberbullied someone else. About 8 percent said they had done so during the previous 30 days.

- Our most recent study found that about 30 percent of teens had been the target of cyberbullying and about 19 percent admitted that they had cyberbullied others—both numbers higher than the 10-year averages.

Other experts have found similar trends. The Crimes Against Children Research Center at the University of New Hampshire, for example, collected data from students across the United States in 2000, 2005, and 2010. They saw a small but steady increase in cyberbullying between 2000 and 2010. So cyberbullying in general appears to be on the rise.

And while most teens are *not* bullying or being bullied, boys and girls of all ages and backgrounds have told us about their experiences with cyberbullying. Girls seem to be just as likely as boys—or a little bit more likely—to be cyberbullied and to cyberbully others. In addition, our survey of more than 4,000 middle and high school students showed that teens from all racial and ethnic backgrounds experience about the same amount of cyberbullying.

The Words We Use
As you read, you'll notice that in some sections of the book we say *he* and *him*, and other times we say *she* and *her*. We've done this to make the book read more smoothly. But *all* the scenarios we talk about can and do happen to anyone, regardless of gender.

Bullying in Person vs. Cyberbullying

One question we get asked a lot is whether technology has created whole new groups of people who bully and are bullied. Think about it: If someone feels tempted to be cruel to someone else, but is afraid of getting caught, chickening out, or being beaten up, he might turn to the Internet, especially if that person is super comfortable using social media and other online tools. On the surface, it seems like there are *plenty* of reasons someone might bully others online but not in real life.

While this way of thinking seems logical, it doesn't appear to be what is actually going on. Most often, those who bully in person also bully online. And those who don't bully in person at school or elsewhere aren't very likely to bully others online, either. Similarly, those who are bullied offline (at school or elsewhere) are more likely to also be bullied online. In fact, one of our surveys found that teens who bullied others in person were more than twice as likely both to be bullied and to bully others online. We also learned that kids who had been bullied in person were almost three times as likely to be cyberbullied.

So bullying in person and bullying online involve many of the same people, and in general they're more similar than they are different. However, they *do* differ in a few important ways:

- One big difference is that <u>targets of cyberbullying don't always know *who* is bullying them.</u> A person who's bullying from behind a computer or cell phone can mask her identity using screen names or anonymous email addresses. However, we've found in our research that many teens who are cyberbullied know (or think they know) exactly who is targeting them. And it's almost always one of their peers, such as a former friend, a former boyfriend or girlfriend, or the new romantic partner of the former boyfriend or girlfriend. And often, if a person being bullied looks closely at what is being said, he will see clues about who is behind it. (Check out **Chapter 3** for more about how someone who is cyberbullying can be identified.)

- Second, **cyberbullying has the potential to go viral** in a way that physical or in-person bullying generally doesn't. A large number of people (at school, in the neighborhood, in the city, and even around the world) can be involved in a cyberbullying incident, or they can at least find out about it with a few taps on a screen or clicks of a mouse. This can make bullying even more painful because it feels like absolutely everyone knows about it. When we were bullied in middle school, only the bully and his buddies were usually there at the time. Afterward, a few classmates might have heard about it—but that was about it. In the case of cyberbullying, though, it's possible for a much larger audience to see or know what happened. This can definitely make cyberbullying much harder to deal with. However, it also means that there are more opportunities for someone to step up and stop the bullying or to stand with the target. That bystander-turned-upstander could be you! (We talk more about what you can do in **Chapter 4**.)

- Third, it is often easier to be cruel online because **cyberbullying can be done from just about anywhere.** That means that the person doing the bullying doesn't always see the effect of his or her words on others. Some people might not even realize or understand the true extent of the pain they are inflicting.

- Fourth, **<u>cyberbullying sometimes goes on for a long time</u>** because many adults don't have the time or technological know-how to keep track of everything that's happening online. This doesn't necessarily mean that they don't care. It's just that they sometimes don't get it, or don't know what to do. Again, this is where you can step in—with the help of what you'll learn from this book.

My best friend and I weren't friends anymore. She was well liked in school, so she ended up turning everyone against me. The bullying first started with girls threatening to jump me and saying that I'd had sex with every guy on the basketball team. I felt betrayed and miserable. Then one day I got on Facebook and there were so many guys asking to be my friend and sending sexual messages to me. I also had girls tagging me in rude pics and comments, and there was a page up that listed all the guys/girls I'd had sex with—but none of it was true. I started not caring about myself and how I dressed or looked. My grades started to drop. I didn't eat lunch because everyone I used to sit with was against me.

—Gabi, 17, Georgia

The Consequences

Bullying is bullying—no matter where it happens. Sometimes, as in Gabi's story, in-person bullying is combined with cyberbullying. Yet even with all the attention focused on cyberbullying, some people don't realize that online hate can be just as hurtful as physical and other in-person bullying. Just because there is no immediate physical harm, and just because people tend to feel free to say things online they would never say face to face, does not mean that it doesn't wound deeply. As we mentioned, sometimes cyberbullying hurts even more, because so many other people are able to see it—and to join

BULLYING IS BULLYING—NO MATTER WHERE IT HAPPENS.

in if they want to. And there's always the fear that the hurtful things said or posted will be out there online forever.

These feelings and other consequences of cyberbullying are serious. Teens who have been cyberbullied say that they feel sad, angry, frustrated, and depressed. Some report having suicidal thoughts. _"It makes me feel really crappy,"_ says Bridget, a 14-year-old in Massachusetts. She adds, _"It makes me walk around the rest of the day feeling worthless, like no one cares. It makes me very, very depressed."_ Michaela of Arizona is 15 years old. She said, _"Being bullied makes me feel like I'm alone in the world. I've cried myself to sleep sometimes."_ Daniel, an 18-year-old from Kentucky, told us, _"The people who bullied me when I was younger made my life a living hell. Because of them, I hated everything, including myself."_ Those who experience cyberbullying have also told us that they were afraid or embarrassed to go to school.

We've also learned that teens affected by cyberbullying (whether they bully or have been bullied) have lower self-esteem and more problems at home and at school. Li, 13, from Oregon said, _"I never knew how serious cyberbullying was until it actually happened to me. When multiple people gang up and point out your flaws, it's the worst feeling ever. To know that multiple people think that way about you ruins your self-esteem, and makes you nervous, self-conscious, and uncomfortable. From now on, those thoughts stay with me."_

People who cyberbully others are also more likely to get into trouble at school and home. That might mean cheating on a test, drinking alcohol, vandalizing property, or running away from home. And some teens who are cyberbullied go on to start bullying others. For example, 14-year-old David from Rhode Island told us, *"I bullied because I was bullied. I said things that weren't true to get the attention away from me. I was hoping that people would forget what they were saying about me and focus on someone else. Instead, I turned into one of them."*

> *I posted a picture of myself on Instagram and people started commenting these awful things like* "Eww ur so ugly" *and* "Why don't you go kill urself everyone would be happier that way." *And I know these people . . . they go to my school! I cried for a good two hours. But this wasn't the first time this happened. On all my pictures at least three people say something like that. I'm never going on Instagram again. I wish I could disappear so I wouldn't have to go to school.*
>
> —Taylor, 14, Colorado

Most Teens Don't Cyberbully

Even though this chapter talks a lot about the ways that some teens hurt others online, it's important to remember that many, many more teens are *not* involved in cyberbullying. That's worth repeating: **Most teens do not cyberbully others!**

Unfortunately, the relatively small number of teens who *do* cyberbully have the potential to mess things up for everyone else. For the most part, they're the ones bringing on the restrictive rules and harsh penalties you've likely heard about or had to deal with. For example, some schools have completely banned all cell phones on campus. Similarly, many schools install software on school computers to prevent students from visiting certain websites—including some that can be useful, such as YouTube. Some adults see the way a few teens act online and assume that many or most act the same way. Then, to try to prevent possible problems, those adults often make rules that affect everyone.

That's one reason why it's in your best interest to speak up and explain to as many people as possible that most teens do not cyberbully, but rather are doing the right things online. And it's up to you to show—through your words and actions—that you and other teens can be safe, smart, kind, and responsible with technology.

Think About It

Q: What are some of the consequences of cyberbullying? Do you know someone who has been targeted? If so, how did it make him or her feel?

Q: A lot of adults think that many, if not most, teens are involved in cyberbullying. Why do you think that most adults have an inaccurate perception of the amount of cyberbullying going on?

??? Status Update: Is It Cyberbullying?

Take a look at the following scenarios and decide whether you think each one is cyberbullying. Why or why not? How would you respond in each situation?

----

1. A friend does not accept your friend request on Facebook.

☐ Yes   ☐ No   ☐ It depends

Things to consider:

* Do you have mutual friends offline? If so, did the person accept their friend requests?
* Do you still hang out with this friend regularly?
* Did you talk to him or her about this?
* How should you respond?

----

2. Someone posts your picture online.

☐ Yes   ☐ No   ☐ It depends

Things to consider:

* Did you give the person permission to take the picture?
* Did you give the person permission to post it online?
* Are you upset by the picture?
* How should you respond?

----

3. Many of your friends from school are posting mean comments on a picture of you on Instagram.

☐ Yes   ☐ No   ☐ It depends

Things to consider:

* Do you feel hurt or embarrassed by what is being said?

----

* Is the situation taking up a lot of space in your mind and seriously bothering you?
* Are the people posting the comments *really* your friends?
* How many people do you estimate have seen the picture and comments?
* How should you respond?

----

4. Another student makes a website about you.

☐ Yes   ☐ No   ☐ It depends

Things to consider:

* Do you feel hurt, embarrassed, or threatened by what is being said on the page?
* Do you know who created this site? If so, do you think the person would remove the page if you asked?
* Do you think the person intended the page to be hurtful?
* How should you respond?

----

5. You receive a text message from a friend that says "You are such a nerd! LOL!"

☐ Yes   ☐ No   ☐ It depends

Things to consider:

* Who sent you the message? Do you consider the person a close friend?
* Has this person ever sent you other texts like this one?
* Did you text him or her first saying something funny?
* How should you respond?

----

6. People have made extremely cruel comments on a video you uploaded to YouTube of you singing and playing guitar.

☐ Yes   ☐ No   ☐ It depends

Things to consider:

* How is it affecting you, emotionally and mentally?
* Does it make you want to stay off YouTube or delete your account?

* How many hurtful comments are there?

* Has anyone said nice things about your video?

* Do you know who made the mean comments? Do their opinions really matter to you?

* How should you respond?

- -

7. Someone signed you up for a bunch of mailing lists, and now you get hundreds of annoying spam emails every single day.

☐ Yes   ☐ No   ☐ It depends

Things to consider:

* Do you know who did it?

* Are you hurt or offended by the emails, or mostly just annoyed?

* Can you easily change your email address without much hassle?

* How should you respond?

- -

8. Someone posts a really gross and offensive picture on Instagram and tags you in it. The caption says, "Tag anyone you know who this picture reminds you of!" A handful of other people you know from school make comments like "LOL," "Hahahaha," and "SO true."

☐ Yes   ☐ No   ☐ It depends

Things to consider:

* Do you know who originally posted and tagged the picture? Is it someone you consider a friend?

* Are you upset, or just annoyed?

* How should you respond?

---

9. Someone sends a tweet with your phone number, telling others to "Call or text for a sexy good time!" It gets retweeted by about 100 other students from your school.

☐ Yes   ☐ No   ☐ It depends

Things to consider:

* Do you know who did it? Do you consider the person a friend? What about the people who are retweeting?
* Are you upset, or mostly just annoyed? Does the tweet seem malicious or more like a joke?
* Do you feel like your safety is at risk?
* How should you respond?

---

10. Someone creates a Tumblr using the nickname everyone knows you use on other social media sites. The person blogs and reblogs memes and videos that refer to homosexuality.

☐ Yes   ☐ No   ☐ It depends

Things to consider:

* Do you know who did it?
* How much do you care about what people think your sexual orientation is (regardless of what it is)?
* Are you upset, or just annoyed?
* In comments, are people being hateful and rude, or mostly just curious and nosy?
* How should you respond?

Chapter 2

What to Do If You're Being Cyberbullied

For the past 8 months I have been cyberbullied. Someone who I thought was my friend started to talk about me. Little by little it just kept getting worse. I'd go online and see things that she and her friend posted about me, and I would just burst out in tears. When summer started things started to die down since we weren't in school anymore. Just when I thought it was over, it started up again. I feel so alone at times. I feel like nobody understands. Every time she and her friend post something online, I don't speak up for myself. I feel like if I try to defend myself they'll twist my words and use them against me. I just don't know what to do anymore.

—Ava, 15, Texas

It hurts a lot to be the target of any kind of bullying. And particularly in the case of cyberbullying, you might feel like there's no escape. After all, a person who's bullying you can say whatever, wherever, whenever—and many other people can see those mean comments and even chime in with their own. Maybe, like Ava, you feel completely alone and believe that no one understands what you're going through. Maybe you think that no one out there can help.

"Being different is always gonna be a tough climb. But at the end of the day, if you give those bullies the power to affect you, you're letting them win. And they don't deserve that."
—*Adam Lambert*

Well, we're here to tell you that there *are* people out there who know and understand what you're going through. There are people who have dealt with similar situations. You are not alone. And—like many others who have experienced this before you—you *can* get through this.

Tools at Your Fingertips

The thousands of teens we've talked to over the years have given us their best suggestions for what to do when being cyberbullied. In this chapter, we'll share those ideas with you. It's important to remember that there isn't one single response that will completely stop all forms of cyberbullying, all of the time. That's why we've given you many different strategies to try, so that you can figure out what works best for you and your situation. The next **10 sections** list **10 ways** to deal with and respond to cyberbullying. You can use these strategies in any order or combination you like. The key is to keep trying and not give up.

1. Keep a Journal

If you're being cyberbullied, one of the most important things you can do is keep a very detailed journal or diary of everything that's happening. If you get to the point where the harassment is too much for you to handle on your own, you'll need to ask for help. But at that point, it might be hard to remember everything that has happened, especially if the cyberbullying has been going on for weeks or months. A journal can help you keep everything straight when you're trying to explain the situation to someone else. Your journal can also give adults the information and details they need to help you.

What to Include in Your Journal

- When did the cyberbullying happen?

- Who did the bullying?

- What did that person do?

- How did you respond?

- Where did it happen? On what website(s)? Using what technology or device (a computer, a cell phone, a tablet, etc.)?

- Did you tell anyone about the bullying? If so, who?

- How is the bullying affecting you—emotionally, mentally, physically, and academically?

- Were you scared for your safety?

Be as specific as you can with the answers to these questions.

Here are two examples of how you might explain and describe cyberbullying that happened to you. The first journal entry is okay, but the second, more detailed one is better.

Okay: *Monday, September 20.* Laura sent me mean text messages today.

Better: *Monday, September 20.* Laura sent me a text at 8:31 tonight that said "the world would be a better place without you in it." I didn't text back. At 8:42 she sent me another message that said "You better not go to school tomorrow." Again, I didn't reply. I haven't told anyone about this because I'm embarrassed, but she's been sending me messages like this for a while now and it's really bothering me. I don't know what to do. I really don't want to see her at school tomorrow. I wish I didn't have to go.

The more details you can include, the better. Sometimes it's hard for adults to understand how painful and frustrating cyberbullying can be. This is a chance for you to explain your side of the story.

To anyone who has been bullied, remember something for me: you're not alone. And it's okay to seek help. You don't have to go through this at all, much less on your own.

—Caleb, 14, Nevada

2. Save the Evidence

One of the things that makes cyberbullying different from other types of bullying is that there is *always* some sort of digital evidence. Whether the harassment happens in the form of a text message, a Facebook comment, an email, a YouTube video, a picture on Instagram, or any other type of online activity, there is always a record of what happened. By contrast, if someone is bullying you in the school hallway, you and that person might be the only ones who know exactly what's going on. And if an adult confronts the person bullying you, it will be your word against his. Getting to the bottom of these kinds of conflicts can be difficult and messy. But when it comes to online bullying, you can show an adult exactly who said what, and when. *If* you keep the evidence, that is.

So as much as you may wish the hurtful messages, pictures, or videos would just disappear, it's important to resist the temptation to delete them immediately. If you do need to turn to an adult for help, it will be much easier for that person to understand what's going on if you can show exactly what was said, sent, or posted. You can save text messages and emails, print out pages from social media profiles, download photos and videos, or take screenshots of anything on a website that you believe to be cyberbullying.

and principal. I was there at the meeting, and it was hard for me to realize that the person bullying me was younger than me. This person continuously would say nasty things about me to my closest and dearest friend, and then to my boyfriend. Thank goodness I have those two and my father. I wouldn't be here if it weren't for them. I had help through this, unlike many teens or kids who are being bullied. The bullying made me depressed and suicidal. I never wanted to do anything or go anywhere. At first I was scared to reach out to someone, but my best friend, boyfriend, and father made me realize that it's not okay to let someone overpower my life. I then took over my life again and now no one has control over me.

—Angelina, 16, Michigan

Think About It

Q: Who do you turn to when you need help or are worried, stressed, sad, or scared? What makes him or her such a good person to talk to?

Q: What do you think adults could do to make it more likely that you would turn to them if you were being cyberbullied?

When to Tell an Adult

In a recent research project, some friends of ours named Stan Davis and Charisse Nixon surveyed nearly 12,000 students from 25 different schools across the United States. They wanted to figure out what works best when responding to bullying. They learned that telling an adult—at home or at school—made things better more often than any other response. If you're being cyberbullied and any of the following descriptions match how you're feeling, don't wait any longer. Tell an adult what's going on if:

- you feel scared
- you're being threatened
- the bullying makes you not want to go to school
- you're avoiding certain people or places at school, and it's having a negative effect on your schoolwork, friendships, or mood
- you find yourself thinking about the situation all the time, and it's negatively affecting your life
- you've tried to get the bullying to stop, but it's still happening
- you are depressed or feel suicidal (if you have suicidal thoughts, you can contact the National Suicide Prevention Lifeline any time at 1-800-273-8255 or **suicidepreventionlifeline.org**)

5. Ignore It

It often seems like people who bully others just want attention or an audience for their actions. The more upset or freaked out you get, the more they get out of the experience. It's sick, but sometimes it's true. So don't give them that satisfaction! If someone is sending you texts that bother you, don't respond. Don't even acknowledge that you got the messages. If the person asks you at school the next day if you got the texts, tell him that you don't know what he's talking about. Hopefully he'll move on. Even if you do ignore the cyberbullying, though, still save copies of the messages, posts, or other evidence so that you can show it to an adult you trust if the bullying doesn't stop.

One of my friends started sending me nasty messages and texts, and this carried on at school. I told my parents, my friends, and a teacher. The girl was spoken to a few times, but it still kept happening. The bullying really affected me at home and at school. I couldn't concentrate on schoolwork and I was always upset and down. Now I just ignore it. I have plenty of other friends and I don't need her anymore. Maybe one day she'll give up and grow up.

—Chandra, 15, United Kingdom

People who make you feel sad, stressed, and mad, and even worried—they really aren't your true friends. True friends wouldn't make you feel uncomfortable, would they? So don't let the small stuff get to you. Good luck! :)

—Ben, 13, New York

6. Laugh It Off

If someone says something funny about you, you could try to laugh it off. Like we said earlier, it *could* be that the person really is just trying to be humorous and doesn't mean to be hurtful. Sometimes people say sarcastic things or poke fun at a friend as a way of connecting with them or to fit in. Plus, it's hard to tell what a person's tone or intent is from words on a screen. Something that would seem like a friendly joke in person can sound really mean online. So, especially if this is the first time the person has acted this way toward you, try to give him the benefit of the doubt. You could even try to give the person something else to laugh about. Respond to the post or comment with a joke or a funny story of your own, and see if that defuses the situation. Even if the person *does* intend to be hurtful, redirecting their humor from you to a joke could help stop the behavior from growing into more serious cyberbullying.

Of course, this strategy isn't always appropriate. If what is said about you really isn't funny at all, and you are sincerely hurt, be honest with yourself and try one of the other responses discussed in this chapter. This technique is only for those times when someone says something about you or a friend that you really think might have been meant as a harmless joke, but which ended up crossing the line.

If people have to insult you through the computer, they aren't worth a second thought.

—Luis, 15, New York

7. Speak Up

If ignoring the bullying doesn't work and the hurtful behavior keeps happening, you can try a different approach: Tell the person to stop. Of course, if you feel very nervous or even scared about doing this, it's not the right strategy for you. But if you do feel like you can speak up, let the person doing the bullying know that what she's doing is hurtful. Another option is to have a good friend step in on your behalf. For example, that friend could say that your feelings are really being hurt by the behavior. There's a chance that the person doing the bullying might think what she's saying or doing is harmless and funny. But if you make it clear that it's seriously bothering you, she might think twice about the behavior, and she may stop.

If you do decide to approach someone who's bullying you, be respectful but firm. Don't act aggressive or angry. Also, you probably don't want to do this in front of a lot of people. That might make the person get defensive. She might try to show off and impress others by making light of the situation or by saying something else mean. You want to give her a fair chance to change her behavior, but you don't want to give her any more positive or negative attention. So try to have this conversation with a few people around, but not necessarily where those other people can hear exactly what you're talking about.

Speaking up is a good step sometimes, but it won't always work. If you talk to the person who's bullying you and the harassment doesn't stop—or if it gets worse—then it's definitely time to get help from an adult.

Finding the Right Words

What can you say to someone who is bullying you online? Here are a few ideas:

- "What you said on Facebook last night was not funny at all to me. I would really appreciate it if you wouldn't say stuff like that anymore."

- "I don't get why you said that about me. Please stop."

- "I know you didn't mean to be mean, but what you said hurt."

- "I would never say anything like that about you, so please don't say things like that about me."

8: Block the Bullying

If someone is repeatedly contacting you online in a way that is distracting, irritating, or hurtful, you should block that person. Most websites and programs such as Facebook, Skype, or Instagram give you the option to block certain users from contacting you or even being able to see whether or not you're online. Many cell phones also have features that let you block or decline calls and texts from certain phone numbers. Or you or your mom or dad can contact your cell phone service provider to help set this up. If certain people can't get in touch with you easily, it will be a lot harder for them to cyberbully you.

Starting when I was 12, I was cyberbullied. That was before people really knew what cyberbullying was. One of my closest friends found that if she made fun of people, other kids thought it was funny, and she got more popular. We had been best friends, but when I wouldn't go along with her in bullying others, she made me her target. She already knew all of my secrets and ways to make fun of me. Soon she turned my friends against me. This was back when AOL instant messenger was really popular, and she used it to harass me even after school. When I blocked her, she would just make new screen names to harass me with. She and her friends made fun of me on MySpace, went after me over AIM, and started rumors about me at school. Finally, after months of this, I went to my parents. At that time, however, there weren't laws against cyberbullying. Fortunately, my parents confronted my former friend's parents, and eventually the bullying stopped. Today, I'm a successful college student, and I have lots of friends who would never do anything like this. There are good people out there. Things get better. Just hold on.

—Karissah, 19, Vermont

9. Report It

Most popular social media and gaming websites allow and encourage users to report malicious comments, inappropriate pictures, and other problems. In fact, cyberbullying violates most sites' terms of service, which generally state that you can't use their pages or features to be cruel or threatening toward someone else. Reporting these issues to the site can help get hurtful content removed quickly—often within 24 to 48 hours. In addition, if a site gets multiple reports about one person, the website administrators may ban the account temporarily or even permanently. Of course, someone could create another account using a different email address. But if they do, and if they continue to bully you, you can report them again. Also, many websites can tell when someone is re-signing up from the same phone or computer, and can block or ban them at that point, too.

Sometimes, before you report somebody to a site, it can be worthwhile to talk to him directly. Let's say Eli posts an Instagram picture of Joe that makes fun of him in some way. It could be that Eli really meant to hurt Joe. But it's also possible that he just wasn't thinking about how Joe might feel when he posted the picture. Joe could contact Instagram and ask the site to contact Eli and pull down the photo. But this strategy can backfire. First off, depending on what the photo shows or what the caption says, the site might not agree to take it down. Facebook, for example, will only remove a photo if it violates the site's terms. Usually that means the photo or its caption contains nudity, hate speech, graphic violence, or similar content.

In addition, being reported might make Eli angry or annoyed— even if what he did *was* wrong. In fact, if Eli gets mad that Joe got him in trouble with the website administrators, he might stubbornly refuse to take down the photo just because he's embarrassed and ticked off. Or he might post more hurtful things. Tension between the two may rise even higher. And all of this *might* stem from a simple mistake that didn't need to blow up into major drama.

Conflicts like the one between Joe and Eli can often be worked out when both people stay calm and rational, and try to solve the problem without getting defensive or aggressive. Joe could start by contacting Eli (online or off) and asking him to take down the picture. He could also explain how it made him feel, and why. Joe might say something like, "I know you probably didn't mean anything by posting this pic, but that's harsh for me. It would mean a lot if you took it down." This friendlier approach doesn't point fingers and won't make Eli feel like the bad guy who has been called

Dealing with Fake Profile Pages

Imagine you get an email from a friend that includes a link to a Twitter account or Facebook profile. You click the link and see your name and picture on the profile. But you didn't create it. And some of the information included isn't exactly flattering. In fact, it's embarrassing and untrue, and it could really hurt your reputation. Now what do you do? Here are a few important steps:

- **Gather as much information** about the fake profile as you can *before* reporting it. Write down the page URL (Web address). Take screenshots or print out the profile and related content, such as pages linked in posts or comments. Try to identify people connected to the profile as friends or followers. Collect their usernames, real names, and contact information if possible. This information can help determine who made the profile, and it can help the site investigate content that might need to be pulled down. But if whoever set up the account deletes it before you have a chance to save evidence, it can be very hard to prove who created it. So it's a good idea to move quickly to capture what you can.

- If you already know who created the page, **respectfully ask the person to remove it**. There's a chance that she doesn't realize that it's making you feel bad. If that's the case, the person may apologize and agree to take down the page.

- If talking to the person who made the page works, great. But if it doesn't—or if you don't know who is behind the profile—**report it.** On Facebook, for example, you can report a fake account—also called an impostor account—by visiting Facebook's Safety Center. You can do this even if you don't have your own Facebook account. If the person who made the fake profile tries to log into the account after you've reported it, Facebook will require the user to prove his or her identity. Facebook will also show the user a map indicating where she is logged in from. This proves to the user that she really *isn't* anonymous.

- **Tell an adult** what's going on and ask for help dealing with the situation.

out. As a result, it's less likely to turn into an even bigger problem. Hopefully Eli will say to himself, "Yeah, I messed up, but I can make things right."

Facebook is one social media platform that encourages person-to-person resolution. The site's features include a special reporting tool that lets you easily and politely ask someone else to take down photos of you or posts about you. Ideally, this will convince the other person to remove whatever he posted that is upsetting you. But if this doesn't work, or if you don't feel comfortable contacting the person, you can still formally report the content to Facebook. Many other websites have similar tools to help you protect your information and reputation.

10. When to Call the Police

As we mentioned earlier, if you feel that any form of cyberbullying puts your safety (or the safety of someone else) in danger, tell an adult right way. He can help decide whether it's time to call the police. An adult can also help you make sure that you've collected the information the police will need to start looking into the situation. The number one goal is to make sure that you and others are safe.

One thing that many people don't realize is that some forms of cyberbullying break the law. Laws vary from place to place, but actions such as stalking, coercion, hate speech, harassment, and invasion of privacy can all land a person in serious trouble. The police won't necessarily respond formally (such as by making an arrest), especially when teens are involved. But getting law enforcement involved can show the person doing the bullying—and his parents—how serious the behavior actually is. It also sends a strong message that if the behavior continues, it could result in stricter discipline and harsher penalties.

Don't Give Up

If you're dealing with hate, harassment, or even just a lot of drama and social stress, don't give up. Try to remember this: *It gets better.* It really does. You might have heard this before. And you might not buy it. When you're in the middle of a bad situation and you feel attacked, it feels like the pain and the problems are never going to go away. Maybe they just seem to get worse and worse. We get that. We've felt it. But we want you to persevere, turn to others (both your friends and the adults in your life) when you need help, and concentrate on becoming the person you want to be. And remember that many people have been where you are, and have ended up even stronger than they were before. Some of them are now successful singers, actors, athletes, and politicians. You are not alone, and it *does* get better.

In fact, a popular movement has helped make this message go viral. Dan Savage and his husband, Terry Miller, started the "It Gets Better" project in 2010. They posted a video to YouTube with a simple message of hope for young people who are being bullied or harassed because of their sexual orientation. "It gets better," Dan said. "However bad it is now, it gets better. And it can get great." Soon, thousands of other people posted their own videos to share their experiences, offer encouragement, and provide support. These people included some of the world's most famous figures, from President Barack Obama to Lady Gaga. The project has grown to inspire and encourage anyone being bullied for any reason. It *will* get better. These people and their stories are evidence of that.

> "To anyone who's being bothered or abused or harassed or bullied . . . I just want to tell you that it will get better."
> —Ke$ha

I've been cyberbullied several times. It still stings. You don't forget it. It hurts, and you wonder, "Why do I deserve this? What did I do?" You question so much about yourself, and whether people really mean what they're saying. So don't even play around or joke. It's not a joke, and it's not funny. Think before you do and think before you say. If you can't say it to someone's face, don't say it at all. And to anyone out there being cyberbullied, it gets better—it sounds like a cliché, but it's true.

—Tomas, 16, Michigan

You're Not to Blame

If you are being mistreated, know that it is not your fault. You didn't do anything to deserve it. No one deserves it. But knowing—and believing—that you're not to blame doesn't make the pain magically go away. After all, it's natural to draw some of your self-worth and sense of identity from the way others think and talk about you. And their opinions *are* going to affect your moods and emotions sometimes. Plus, people often tend to be their own worst critics. Maybe you're really hard on yourself about a million different things. If others point out or make fun of something you're already sensitive or insecure about, it can make you feel even worse.

On top of all that, a big part of this time in your life is figuring out who you are and what you want. You're working on becoming more comfortable with yourself, and you're working toward your hopes and dreams. Plus, you're dealing with all kinds of stresses and challenges at school, at home, and with friends. That's a lot going on. Life probably feels a bit unstable at times, like it could fall apart any moment. So when somebody mistreats or embarrasses you, it can be really hard to tell yourself that you shouldn't let it bother you, and that you just need to shrug it off. It's not that easy. Nobody wants to be rejected, disrespected, or humiliated.

The important thing is to try not to let your identity be *completely* wrapped up in how others see you and what they say about you. This isn't easy, either! And it doesn't help that people's opinions and feelings change all the time. Remember that pair of jeans you loved once, but don't really want to wear anymore? Remember that movie star you had a crush on, but now are totally over? Remember that band whose older songs you were crazy about, but whose newer stuff you don't like at all? Our perceptions, likes, dislikes, preferences, and tastes are always evolving. That's how it is for everybody. So it's no wonder that sometimes it feels like there's just no pleasing others!

> "Being a teenager and figuring out who you are is hard enough without someone attacking you."
> —*Ellen DeGeneres*

People can dislike you for being unattractive (in their opinion), and they can dislike you for being very attractive. People can bully you for being not smart (in their opinion), or for being really smart. It seems like people can come up with any reason to justify—in their own minds—judging others or treating them badly. So if your identity is totally dependent on what *other* people are thinking and saying, your own well-being and happiness will be at the mercy of those thoughts and feelings and opinions and demands—all of which are changing constantly. That's an awful way to live.

Naturally, it's still going to hurt when someone says something cruel to you or about you. But with time, you can get better and better at not letting these comments rule your life. You can work on basing your feelings about yourself on the things and people *you* care about—*your* passions, goals, and values. You can talk positively to yourself, rather than putting yourself down. And you can remember that you can't control what other people do, think, or say—as much as you might want to.

Thoughts of Suicide

Cyberbullying can take over your world. When it gets really rough, it can make you lose focus on the good things in your life—the family and friends who love you, the knowledge that you have unique talents and abilities, and the fact that you have a future filled with unknown opportunities once you get through these tough times. Being bullied can make you want to stay under your bedcovers and never come out. It can make you want to completely shut out everyone and everything. And it might feel like there's no escape. When you feel that desperate and unhappy, you might even think about taking your own life.

If you're at that point, *get help*. Tell someone right away. You can talk to someone you know—a parent, a friend, a teacher, or anyone else you trust. Or call a hotline such as the National Suicide Prevention Lifeline (**suicidepreventionlifeline.org** or 1-800-273-8255). The caring and compassionate people there are available 24 hours a day, 7 days a week, and they'll do whatever they can to help you.

Similarly, if you're worried that someone else is suicidal, don't dismiss your concern. Trust your gut and tell someone who can try to do something about it. If you see a warning sign online, you can contact the website where the worrying post appeared. Some of these online warning signs that could indicate suicidal thoughts include:

- Writing or posting about suicide or death, even if the person seems to be joking about it

- Frequently using hashtags that relate to sadness, loneliness, hopelessness, failure, giving up, suicide, or death
- Posting status updates, captions, comments, pictures, or videos that are very dark and depressing

You might also see warning signs in person. Some of these might be:

- Mood swings
- A person withdrawing and isolating himself or herself
- Someone losing interest in things that previously brought him or her joy
- Giving away possessions, especially those with a lot of meaning
- Extreme sadness, hopelessness, and resignation

If you see something that worries you, take action. If the person you're concerned about is at school or in your community, tell an adult you trust. You can also notify websites of warning signs online. Twitter, Tumblr, Facebook, YouTube, and other social media sites have clear and quick response systems whenever someone alerts them about a person on the site who seems to be considering suicide. They don't take any chances, and neither should you.

One of my friends killed himself because of bullying. I vowed then never to hurt anyone—to their face, or behind their back.

—Charles, 15, Louisiana

Stay Strong

There may not be a single, magical solution that will stop cyberbullying, but there *are* many different ways to respond if you're being cyberbullied. You might find out that one of the strategies in this chapter worked in one situation but not in another. Talk to friends and see what has worked for them. Don't give up. Remember, it *will* get better. Eventually the bullying will stop. And the ideas in this chapter can help make that happen sooner than later.

Think About It

Q: What do you think is the most effective way to respond to cyberbullying? Have you tried something that isn't mentioned here, but that worked well for you? If so, what was it?

Q: If a younger student were being cyberbullied and asked you for help, what would you tell the person? How would you try to help?

Status Update: Are You Being Cyberbullied?

Have you been cyberbullied? Answer these questions, add up your points, and then read about your score. Did you learn anything that surprised you? If so, what will you do next?

----

1. Someone wrote something about me on a social networking website that was mean or hurtful.

☐ **Never**: 0 points   ☐ **Once or twice**: 1 point   ☐ **Many times**: 2 points

----

2. I stayed home from school because of something mean that was said about me online.

☐ **Never**: 0 points   ☐ **Once or twice**: 1 point   ☐ **Many times**: 2 points

----

3. Someone intentionally posted a humiliating picture or video of me online.

☐ **Never**: 0 points   ☐ **Once or twice**: 1 point   ☐ **Many times**: 2 points

----

4. Someone created a fake online profile about me that upset me or hurt my feelings.

☐ **Never**: 0 points   ☐ **Once or twice**: 1 point   ☐ **Many times**: 2 points

----

5. I stayed off social media for a while because I was tired of seeing some of the things people were saying about me.

☐ **Never**: 0 points   ☐ **Once or twice**: 1 point   ☐ **Many times**: 2 points

----

----

6. I received a text message from someone I didn't know that was really mean or hurtful.

☐ **Never**: 0 points   ☐ **Once or twice**: 1 point   ☐ **Many times**: 2 points

----

7. Someone spread rumors about me online.

☐ **Never**: 0 points   ☐ **Once or twice**: 1 point   ☐ **Many times**: 2 points

----

8. A friend has told me that another classmate was saying cruel things about me online.

☐ **Never**: 0 points   ☐ **Once or twice**: 1 point   ☐ **Many times**: 2 points

----

9. Someone threatened to hurt me through a text message or online, and I was definitely scared.

☐ **Never**: 0 points   ☐ **Once or twice**: 1 point   ☐ **Many times**: 2 points

----

10. Someone pretended to be me online and acted in a way that was mean or that got me in trouble.

☐ **Never**: 0 points   ☐ **Once or twice**: 1 point   ☐ **Many times**: 2 points

Total:

SCORING

0 points: It doesn't sound like you've ever been cyberbullied—at least not in any of the most common ways. That's great—although it does mean that it might be hard for you to imagine how it feels to be targeted. Talk to your friends and classmates, and ask if any of them have been through it. If they have, **Chapter 4** will give you some ideas and tips for how to help.

1–10 points: You probably aren't being cyberbullied. (Remember, a big part of bullying is the fact that it is repeated.) Or if you have experienced online bullying a few times, maybe it hasn't bothered you all that much. Still, some of the stuff being posted does get to you sometimes. You wish it would stop, but maybe aren't quite sure what to do. Even if you're dealing with a milder bullying situation, the ideas in this chapter will still work for you.

11–20 points: You're dealing with cyberbullying. You're not alone—about one in four teens has been cyberbullied. This book is full of practical ideas to help you address the problem. And hopefully you have a friend or an adult in your life who you can talk to about what you are going through. It's even harder to deal with these kinds of things by yourself. So reach out to others and get the help you need.

Part Two

Treating Others with Respect and Protecting Yourself

Chapter 3

Pause Before You Post

Every day I'm bullied on YouTube. I'm told that my voice sucks *and that* I'm a stalker *because I love Justin Bieber and posted a video about how much I love him. And on Instagram they call me a* stupid b**** *for standing up for Amanda Todd! I love her and she inspired me to post a video called the Sophie Project to Stop Bullying. But even today I get called names and made fun of all the time. No one should have to go through the pain I've gone through. Cyberbullying must stop!*

—Sophie, 13, Ohio

In **Chapter 2**, we talked about what to do if you're being cyberbullied. In this chapter, we'll talk about why it's crucial to always use technology in smart, safe, and responsible ways. It seems like cell phones, computers, and tablets are everywhere—which means that just about anyone has the opportunity to cyberbully others anytime and anyplace. Sometimes it starts as a joke and develops into something very serious. Other times, it happens because someone is mad or hurt, and acts without thinking about what might happen later. Or, maybe your friends have tried to talk you into bullying someone else online as a dare or because they think it would be funny or cool. However it starts, cyberbullying doesn't end well. It can have serious, real-world consequences, from hurt feelings and broken friendships to punishment at home, at school, or even in court.

Think First

In our work, we've found that there's one very simple suggestion that can keep most online conflicts and misunderstandings from flaring up into full-blown cyberbullying: *think before you click*. It may not sound like much, but it really works. Try never to post or respond to anything online when you're angry or upset—even if it's just a little, and *especially* if it's a lot. Close your Web browser. Step away from your computer. Put down your phone. Give yourself a few hours, or even a day or two, to think through the best action or response. Quickly reacting based on emotion almost never resolves a problem. Often, it makes things worse. That's why it's important to spend some time thinking about what you can do to control your actions when anger threatens to get the better of you.

Talk to other people about this, too. Ask some of your friends and family members if they've ever regretted saying something when they were really worked up, instead of calming down first. They'll probably say yes. *We* would! We've both definitely regretted speaking out in a moment of anger, frustration, or hurt feelings, when we really should have cooled down first. When you take a step back and then approach the situation with a level head, things will almost always turn out a lot better.

> *I'm not gonna lie, I've said some stuff over Facebook to my friend like you're this and that, and cussing at her because I was angry that she was going out with my ex-boyfriend. My mom got really mad when she found out what I did. I felt bad, too, but at first it wasn't because I said all those mean things—it was because I got caught! But then I learned that I was a bully and what I did was really wrong.*
>
> —Jasmine, 14, Tennessee

Act with Integrity—Online and Off

It's *always* a good idea to use phones, computers, and other technology responsibly and with integrity. Keith Nord, a former walk-on football player who became a captain of the Minnesota Vikings and then a motivational speaker, says that having integrity means doing the right thing even when it costs you. It might cost you money, time, or your reputation. It might even cost you a friend. But doing the right thing *no matter what* is a mark of true character.

When it comes to the way you act online, acting with integrity might mean not letting your friends or others pressure you into doing something you know is wrong, whether it's sending a mean text or sharing a photo to embarrass somebody. Or, maybe you see a friend constantly making nasty comments to someone online. You know you should say something, yet you're afraid of losing her as a friend. But anyone who is cruel to others could turn out to be cruel to you, too. Who needs friends like that? And if *you're* the one being cruel, people won't want to be your friend either.

Sometimes, you might be thinking about cyberbullying someone not because you're afraid of losing something, but because you think it will help you in some way. You might want to get revenge. Or maybe you think you can earn respect from someone by putting another person down. You might

Think About It

Q: Have you ever posted, texted, or emailed someone when you were hurt or angry? What happened?

Q: Consider some ways you can cool down when you're fired up. For example, you could take a walk, write in a journal, listen to music, call your best friend, or go to the gym. What works for you?

do it because it feels like a way to release stress or anger. Maybe it helps you move the spotlight onto someone else, so that you aren't the one being targeted. But in all of these situations, you're sacrificing your integrity. Deep down inside, you know that what you're about to do is wrong. So trust your better judgment. It will guide you to the right decision.

(A nice side effect of doing the right thing is that most adults in your life will take note of how you act and have more trust in you to be responsible. Then they probably won't feel like they need to be in your online business all the time. And that just makes life easier.)

> "It is our choices, Harry, that show what we truly are, far more than our abilities."
> —*Professor Dumbledore in* Harry Potter and the Chamber of Secrets *by J.K. Rowling*

Don't Let Differences Divide

If you pay attention to the world around you, you know that everyone's different. Physically, we're different in lots of ways, from hair color to height. We're also different in endless ways beyond appearance: our musical taste, clothing style and preference, family, social group, heritage, religious background, political leanings, favorite activities, books, movies, shows—even the way we think, talk, act, and make choices.

These differences—*any* differences—should never be reasons why someone is treated better or worse than someone else. No one is better or worse than someone else; no one has less or more value than anyone else. Nevertheless, disrespect for differences can be one cause of bullying and cyberbullying. For example, someone might bully a classmate because his parents are divorced, or because he doesn't do well in gym class.

Work on stopping this kind of bullying at its source. Remind yourself and others of everyone's similarities instead of differences.

Make a point of catching yourself (and stopping yourself) when you feel yourself judging someone who is different from you. Just as you have to pull weeds out of a garden by their roots, finding the root of these thoughts and emotions can help get rid of them for good, so they won't crop up again later. Talk about this with your friends, too, so they can start understanding their own mindsets and assumptions about others.

Think About It

Q: Has anyone ever discriminated against you or been prejudiced toward you or a friend for some reason? If so, how did that feel? How often do you think these kinds of feelings are related to bullying?

Q: Have you ever caught yourself making a snap judgment or an unkind assumption about someone, even if you didn't really know him or her? If so, did you think about why you did this, and did you try to change your mindset going forward?

Watch Your Words

When we talk to teens who admit that they've cyberbullied others, one thing we hear a lot is that they were "just joking around." Sometimes, the people doing the bullying think they're just having fun and don't think it's that big of a deal. But online or offline, what one person says as a joke could actually be a *very* big deal—and not funny at all—to the person on the receiving end. So at what point does a comment cross the line into being abusive and hurtful? This can be a hard question to answer, since what's funny to one person could be extremely painful or offensive to another depending on his or her personality, sense of humor, self-esteem, and current situation or mood.

For example, you might make jokes about yourself by calling yourself a nerd, or patting your stomach and kidding about your "food baby" after a big meal. This can be funny when you're just focusing on yourself, but if you point out the same thing in someone else, it can come across as mean and embarrassing. How well you know the person also makes a difference. Your best friend might think it's hilarious (and know that you're only joking) when you call her a geek for always acing her math tests, but someone you don't know very well might be insulted.

Reading people's feelings, interpreting their behaviors and responses, and knowing when to back off or apologize can be hard enough when you're talking in the same room. Online, it gets even more difficult and complicated. A gentle, joking tone that you might use in person isn't always clear in a tweet, an email, or a comment on a picture. The person you're talking to or about simply might not be able to tell whether you're launching an attack or just poking some good-natured fun. She might get really mad and hurt. Plus, in person you can probably tell from someone's body language and expressions if she is really getting upset, so you know if it's time to cut it out or say you're sorry. Online, you can't see those signs to guide you.

Another thing to remember when you're behind a keyboard or touchscreen is that many people might see a comment you make to someone else. Would you tell that joke in a crowded cafeteria where lots of people could hear you? Would you say that to a person at a party or a school basketball game, in front of everyone? If not, you probably shouldn't say it online, either—even though you might *feel* anonymous, invisible, or powerful. You might feel free to say and do whatever you want. And the distance between you and the other person can fool you into thinking that what happens in cyberspace doesn't have any real-world consequences. But the truth is very different. Lines are easily crossed, and many statements that were meant to be mildly sarcastic or humorous can end up doing a ton of damage. So think carefully about your words before you post, comment, email, or text.

What Your School Can Do

You probably already know that if you bully someone at school, school officials can discipline you. Forty-nine U.S. states (all except Montana) have laws requiring schools to have anti-bullying policies. These policies often lay out various punishments for students who harass others on campus. But what about cyberbullying? You might think that because it happens online, it isn't the school's responsibility or right to get involved, especially if it didn't take place while you were on school property. But that's not the case. Your principal, teachers, and school administrators do have specific roles and responsibilities when it comes to your online activities. In fact, almost all state bullying laws have been updated to include specific references to cyberbullying. For example, New Hampshire law says: _"The school board of each school district shall adopt a written policy prohibiting bullying, harassment, intimidation, and cyberbullying."_ In California, the law states that _"bullying, including bullying committed by means of an electronic act"_ can lead to suspension or expulsion.

Kara Kowalski found this out firsthand. She was a senior at Musselman High School in West Virginia when she created a MySpace discussion group (a popular online forum at the time)

Making Changes

You might be someone who cyberbullied others in the past. Or maybe you still do bully others, but you really want to quit. It can be hard to change when you're used to acting a certain way. Here are a few ideas to help you stop bullying and to prevent you from going back to those same habits.

- Start each day reminding yourself of the reasons you want to change your habits, rise above the drama and hate, and be a kinder person.
- Walk away from the computer or put down your phone when you feel tempted to say something cruel or embarrassing.
- Consider how you'd feel if someone else treated you that way, for any reason.
- Think of ways to cool down when you feel stressed or when you're angry at someone. You could call a friend, play sports, go for a walk, listen to music, or take a shower. Then you can calmly figure out how to deal with the situation.
- Limit the amount of time you spend with friends who encourage bullying, teasing, and other unkind behavior.
- If you do slip up, remind yourself that everyone makes mistakes. You can still keep working to build better habits.
- Apologize to the person or people you've mistreated. It won't change what you originally did, but it will help you—and those you've hurt—move on.
- Stand up for others when you see bullying happen.
- If you feel angry, sad, or anxious a lot of the time, talk to an adult you trust.

criticizing one of her classmates. Kara made the page at home, on her personal computer. Soon after the page went up, several other Musselman students joined the group. Some of them were at school when they joined or commented on the page. When the targeted student complained to the school, the investigation identified Kara as the student responsible for creating it. She was suspended from school for five days and she also got a 90-day "social suspension" barring her from participating in the school's extra-curricular activities. Later, when a federal appeals court reviewed the case, they supported the school's response. Even though the site was created outside the school walls, the court decided it disrupted the learning environment *at* school, which meant that the school had the right to discipline Kara.

Other students have also gotten in trouble for online activities that happened away from school. Austin Carroll, a senior from Garrett, Indiana, was expelled from school just a few months before graduation for tweeting: *"f*** is one of those f***ing words you can f***ing put anywhere in a f***ing sentence and it still f***ing makes sense."*

Chris Latour, a student from Massachusetts, was expelled during his senior year for publicly posting the password to his English teacher's Edmodo site, which she used to communicate with her students. When Chris shared her password, many students posted sexually offensive and threatening content on the page. This created such a hostile environment for the teacher that she needed medical care for stress and emotional harm. Yuri Wright, another senior and a nationally recognized football star, was expelled from his private school in New Jersey when his inappropriate tweets— which were racially and sexually offensive—came to the attention of school officials. Yuri also lost several scholarship opportunities to play Division I college football with some of the best teams in the nation. These are just a few examples of students who have faced serious consequences at school (and beyond) for what they posted online.

Know Your Rights

In the United States, the Constitution and its amendments guarantee important rights. The U.S. Supreme Court has interpreted these amendments in different ways over the years. The court's decisions, in addition to existing anti-bullying laws, affect you at home, at school, and online. In this section, we'll discuss the rights that are most relevant to you and your words—in cyberspace and beyond.

First Amendment

"Congress shall make no law respecting an establishment of religion, or prohibiting the free exercise thereof; or abridging the freedom of speech, or of the press; or the right of the people peaceably to assemble, and to petition the Government for a redress of grievances."

The First Amendment to the United States Constitution gives you the right (among others) to free speech—the right to speak your mind and share your opinions. Posting your thoughts or ideas online is a form of speech that is often protected by this amendment. Having the right to free speech, however, doesn't mean that you can say whatever you want, whenever you want. For instance, the First Amendment doesn't give you the right to threaten, harass, or intimidate someone. In 1969, the Supreme Court said that students "do not shed their free speech rights at the schoolhouse gate" (*Tinker v. Des Moines Independent Community School District*). But the court also said that special rules apply to teachers and other educators. They have a responsibility and a right to maintain an appropriate and safe learning environment at school. That may include disciplining students for their actions on the Internet.

For example, the Supreme Court has put restrictions on what students can say about school officials—online or off. You have the right to criticize your teachers and other officials, but there are limits. If a student criticizes a teacher in a way that interferes with teaching and learning at school, then the school has the authority to formally discipline the student with detention, suspension, or even expulsion. Your school can also discipline you in less serious ways, such as calling your parents or requiring you to meet with the principal. You can even be kicked off sports teams or out of clubs.

Even if what you're doing doesn't disrupt learning enough for you to be disciplined by your school, your parents could still find out about your behavior online and ground you, take away privileges, or punish you in some other way. In addition, if you say something really mean, offensive, or false about another person, or if you invade someone's privacy, that person might sue you in court. That could result in you (or your family) having to pay that person a lot of money. For instance, a court ordered an 8th grader in Pennsylvania to pay $500,000 to the target of his online threats.

In short, just because you *can* say or post something doesn't mean you *should*. It could have serious consequences for you and for the person you're talking about.

Think About It

Q: Do you think the First Amendment means that you have the right to say whatever you want about another student at your school? Or about teachers? Why or why not?

Fourth Amendment

"The right of the people to be secure in their persons, houses, papers, and effects, against unreasonable searches and seizures, shall not be violated, and no Warrants shall issue, but upon probable cause, supported by Oath or affirmation, and particularly describing the place to be searched, and the persons or things to be seized."

The Fourth Amendment to the U.S. Constitution protects you from "unreasonable searches and seizures." That means that a police officer or other government agents or employees can't just seize (take) or search you or your property whenever they want to. They need to have a justifiable reason to do it. For police specifically, it is "reasonable" to search a person or his or her home or property if there is *probable cause* (reasonable suspicion and supporting information) that the person has committed a crime or is planning to, and if the police believe that a search will find evidence of that behavior or plan.

Essentially, the U.S. Supreme Court has interpreted this amendment as saying that your privacy should not be compromised unless there is a good, legal reason to do so. And the amount of government intrusion allowed depends on the situation. For example, the police can approach and ask you questions more often when you're in a public place than when you're at home or on other private property. Clearly, you would expect to have lots of privacy (not only from the police!) in your bathroom at home, but not so much on a park bench.

So how could this apply to your online activity? Do you have the right to privacy on your cell phone, laptop, or another portable electronic device while you're at school? The short answer is yes— and no. For example, if you've violated a school rule or policy about using a cell phone at school, school staff can legally take the phone away, and you may be punished for breaking the rules. Your parents might have to come to school to get the phone back. You also might be required to write a paper or even pay a fine.

Once a phone or other device is taken, the next question is whether your school has the authority to *search* it. That depends on a lot of factors, but again it comes back to "reasonableness." A 1985 Supreme Court case confirmed that students are protected by the Fourth Amendment. But the court also went on to say that educators don't have to follow *all* the same rules that police do. In general, the standard applied to school officials is whether the search is "justified" and "reasonable in scope." This is fancy legal-talk for "it depends." It depends on what you were doing, and it depends on whether your teacher or principal had a valid reason to believe that you were violating school policy about cell phones and other devices.

For example, if your history teacher has a good reason to think that you're cheating on a quiz by looking at answers on your phone, he could take your phone away. Or if the principal finds out about texts you've sent harassing another student and concludes that you're cyberbullying, she may have the authority to search your phone. In cases like these, the school would probably call your parents, too. School officials might even get the police involved if they think you've done something that breaks the law.

Answering to the Police

Your school clearly has the right to punish you for cyberbullying, even if you've done it from home. But when could it move to the next level? At what point do the police get involved? While laws about this vary depending on location, some types of online harassment definitely qualify as crimes. In Wisconsin, for instance, it's a crime to *"frighten, intimidate, threaten, abuse or harass another person"* through email or any other *"computerized communication system."* *It's also a crime to "expose [another person] to hatred, contempt, ridicule, degradation or disgrace."* Similar laws exist in other states. School officials regularly work with law enforcement to determine whether cyberbullying rises to the level of a crime. If they believe it does, you may find yourself answering your front door to the knocks of a police officer. That's what happened to Keeley Houghton, an 18-year-old in England. After having an argument with Emily Moore, a girl she knew from school, Keeley threatened Emily on Facebook. She posted, "Keeley is going to murder the b****. . . . Emily F***head Moore." Keeley was found guilty of harassment and jailed for three months.

Keeley later expressed regret for her actions. She also said that she'd been warned she could be sent to prison for cyberbullying, but she didn't really think it would actually happen. But it did.

A kid from my school was always bullying the mentally disabled students, so two of my friends and I decided we needed to do something about it. The kid that did the bullying put his whole life into his YouTube channel, so we decided we would try and show him what it feels like to be bullied. We posted all this abuse on his YouTube page—pages and pages of it. Afterward we felt pretty good and mighty. But a few days later, we had to go into the police station because he had reported us for cyberbullying. We all ended up with 20 hours of community service. Plus, the story has another side. Because that kid didn't stop bullying, all his friends left him, and now he has no one to hang around with. In the end, none of us won. Don't try to fight fire with fire, because everyone will end up getting burnt.

—Simon, 16, Australia

Taking It to Court

The following court cases are some of the ones that have informed the ability and right of schools to intervene and discipline students for cyber-bullying, even when it takes place off-campus.

Tinker v. Des Moines Independent Community School District (1969): This famous case concluded that students do have free-speech rights at school. "A prohibition against expression of opinion, without any evidence that the rule is necessary to avoid substantial interference with school discipline or the rights of others, is not permissible under the First and Fourteenth Amendments." Students have constitutional rights under the First Amendment. Those rights, however, do not grant students the right to substantially interfere with school discipline or the "the rights of other students to be secure and to be let alone."

New Jersey v. T.L.O. (1985): This important case found that searches of student property can be conducted by school administrators if there is a reasonable suspicion that a school policy or law has been violated. This standard is less strict than the probable cause standard for searches by the police in settings other than school. The court stated that the rights of children and teens are not the same as those of adults, and that school officials have a responsibility to maintain the discipline necessary for education. Therefore, a "school official may properly conduct a search of a student's person if the official has a reasonable suspicion that a crime has been . . . committed, or reasonable cause to believe that the search is necessary to maintain school discipline."

Bethel School District No. 403 v. Fraser (1986): This case stated that there are some limits to a student's free-speech rights at school, saying that "the constitutional rights of students in public school are not automatically coextensive with the rights of adults in other settings." The Supreme Court ruled that there is an important difference between nondisruptive expression and "speech or action that intrudes upon the work of the schools or the rights of other students."

Davis v. Monroe County Board of Education (1999): This case concluded that if a school knows about harassment or other hurtful actions against students and doesn't respond effectively to stop it, the school and its officials may be held responsible. It said, in part, "the common law, too, has put schools on notice that they may be held responsible under state law for their failure to protect students from the ... acts of third parties."

J.S. v. Bethlehem Area School District (2000): This case about a student who created a website threatening his algebra teacher determined that schools can discipline students for their off-campus electronic speech—*especially* if it's threatening. The court's decision read, in part, "school officials are justified in taking very seriously threats against faculty and other students."

Wisniewski v. Board of Education of Weedsport Central School District (2007): This case was about Aaron Wisniewski, an 8th grader who created an instant messaging buddy icon showing a gun firing at a man's head, and including the words "Kill Mr. VanderMolen" (one of Aaron's teachers). The court declared, "the fact that Aaron's creation and transmission of the icon occurred away from school property does not necessarily insulate him from school discipline. We have recognized that off-campus conduct can create a foreseeable risk of substantial disruption within a school."

Kowalski v. Berkeley County Schools (2011): The court decided in Kara Kowalski's case that schools can discipline students for their online speech, within certain boundaries (including those established by the 1969 *Tinker* case). The court said, "Kowalski used the Internet to orchestrate a targeted attack on a classmate, and did so in a manner that was sufficiently connected to the school environment as to implicate the School District's recognized authority to discipline speech which 'materially and substantially interfere[es] with the requirements of appropriate discipline in the operation of the school and collid[es] with the rights of others.' "

For more information about cyberbullying, the laws, and their effect on you, check out *Teen Cyberbullying Investigated: Where Do Your Rights End and Consequences Begin?* by Judge Tom Jacobs.

Tracing Digital Footprints

Posting, commenting, and other activities online seem to fall into a weird space between two worlds. On the one hand, they can give you and your thoughts a lot of visibility. At the same time, they offer you the chance to seem anonymous. This means that others—possibly many others—can see your thoughts without actually seeing *you*. You can express your ideas in a relatively safe but still public way.

We know that technology has made it much easier to *appear* to post something without others discovering who's behind it. You can use a screen name, a temporary email address, or other tools to conceal your identity. But in fact, just about everything sent or posted on the Internet can be traced back to the original poster. Everything online has what is called a "digital footprint." Law officers, computer experts, and others can discover this footprint and then use it to track where online content came from (who wrote or posted it, when, and from where). In some cases, judges have ordered websites such as Google and Facebook to identify and reveal users accused of cyberbullying. This is possible even if a person used fake information to set up the account.

In other cases, online posters have been tracked down by others who visit the same site. For example, in 2012 a Burger King employee posted a photo of himself on the website 4chan. The picture showed him standing on two tubs of the restaurant's lettuce, and the caption read, *"This is the lettuce you eat at Burger King."* He must have assumed that 4chan regulars would find the photo hilarious. But he was wrong. It turned out that many viewers liked to eat at Burger King, and they were shocked and grossed out by the photo. So they decided to take matters into their own hands and teach this unsanitary employee a lesson. Most digital cameras and cell phones attach information called metadata (also called exif data) to the photos they take. Metadata includes date and time information, camera settings, and sometimes location information. In this case, the metadata pointed to where the picture was taken. Within 15 minutes, 4chan users knew what city the restaurant was in. Plus, one clever user noticed a bar code on a box in the photo's background and thought it would help Burger King managers know exactly which restaurant location was shown. A quick investigation led to three employees who were involved, and they were immediately fired. Although this situation isn't specifically an example of cyberbullying, it *does* clearly show how a post that seems anonymous is actually anything but.

Another person who thought he could hide behind a computer screen was a 16-year-old boy at a high school in the Midwest. First he posted a series of inappropriate tweets criticizing how his fellow students lived and acted. The school's principal tracked any mention of the school's name on Twitter, so when he spotted the tweets, he got worried. He contacted us (and Twitter) right away. Shortly afterward, the student posted a video on YouTube. It showed an image of the masked face from the movie *V for Vendetta*. While the image was on-screen, a computer-generated voice stated:

"I am not here to physically harm anyone here . . . or the school itself. I am not as stupid as you think. I just wanted to let you all know how you live your lives is dangerous and wrong and you have grown weak-minded and pathetic. These are a few mistakes you make every day. Next time we meet I will have something more interesting to show you all. Have a great day."

The video made the local news, alarming many people in the community. Hundreds called the police to ask for information and reassurance. The student quickly posted a second video, again saying that he wouldn't hurt anyone. But the damage was done.

This student was good with computers, and he took several steps to disguise his identity and location. However, the police began an investigation and worked with YouTube to track the digital footprint of the video uploads. They soon identified the person behind the posts. The student was expelled from school and also given a misdemeanor for inducing panic. He may or may not have been joking around, but either way, the incident has the potential to follow him for the rest of his life. Sometimes one incident, even if you've tried to think it through and cover your tracks, can do real damage to your future. Cyberbullying and other irresponsible behaviors online just aren't worth the risk.

Use Your Head (and Your Heart)

Cyberbullying can lead to all kinds of consequences—for your reputation, at school, at home, and even with the police. And some of these consequences can follow you for years. Life is hard enough as it is! Don't make it even harder for you to reach your goals and achieve your dreams because you made a shortsighted decision and got caught.

> "Always do right. This will gratify some people and astonish the rest."
> —*Mark Twain*

Wherever bullying leads, it usually starts from a simple but destructive place: when we forget or choose not to treat others how we'd like to be treated. It can be easy to make excuses sometimes—"I had a bad day" or "He was a jerk to me first." But there aren't any *good* excuses for cyberbullying. Remember how much it hurts you when people ignore, reject, embarrass, or make fun of you. Think about how you'd feel if someone did the same thing to your best friend, brother, sister, mom, or dad. Work on not distancing yourself from the pain cyberbullying can cause, and try not to fall into a "me vs. them" mentality. Having that mentality is a horrible way to live. It can harden your heart toward others. Sometimes it can lead to tragedy.

We've said it before and we'll say it again: Pause before you post, and step away if you need to. It works, and it can save you—and others—a lot of headaches and heartaches.

Status Update: Do You Cyberbully?

As you've read this chapter, you might have thought to yourself that you would never cyberbully anyone. But are you sure? Some things that you might not think are cyberbullying could cross the line. Take this quiz to find out if you've participated in any form of cyberbullying. If you have, think about what you'll do to change your habits or to prevent cyberbullying in the future.

----

1. I've written something mean or hurtful about someone on social media.

☐ **Never**: 0 points   ☐ **Once or twice**: 1 point   ☐ **Many times**: 2 points

----

2. I've "liked" or added a funny comment to someone else's online post that was hurtful toward another person.

☐ **Never**: 0 points   ☐ **Once or twice**: 1 point   ☐ **Many times**: 2 points

----

3. I've made or shared a video that was embarrassing or humiliating about someone else.

☐ **Never**: 0 points   ☐ **Once or twice**: 1 point   ☐ **Many times**: 2 points

----

4. I've created a fake profile online for the purpose of making fun of someone else.

☐ **Never**: 0 points   ☐ **Once or twice**: 1 point   ☐ **Many times**: 2 points

----

5. I've threatened to hurt someone in a text message.

☐ **Never**: 0 points   ☐ **Once or twice**: 1 point   ☐ **Many times**: 2 points

----

----

6. A parent or an adult from school has told me that what I was doing was cyberbullying.

☐ **Never**: 0 points   ☐ **Once or twice**: 1 point   ☐ **Many times**: 2 points

----

7. I've sent a text that I knew was mean or offensive.

☐ **Never**: 0 points   ☐ **Once or twice**: 1 point   ☐ **Many times**: 2 points

----

8. I've seen someone from my school being cyberbullied and I didn't do anything to stop it.

☐ **Never**: 0 points   ☐ **Once or twice**: 1 point   ☐ **Many times**: 2 points

----

9. I've encouraged my friends to say something mean online about another person.

☐ **Never**: 0 points   ☐ **Once or twice**: 1 point   ☐ **Many times**: 2 points

----

10. I've gotten in trouble at school or with my parents because of cyberbullying.

☐ **Never**: 0 points   ☐ **Once or twice**: 1 point   ☐ **Many times**: 2 points

----

11. I've forwarded something (like an email or text) that spread mean rumors about someone else.

☐ **Never**: 0 points   ☐ **Once or twice**: 1 point   ☐ **Many times**: 2 points

----

12. I've joined or liked a group or a page that makes fun of someone.

☐ **Never**: 0 points   ☐ **Once or twice**: 1 point   ☐ **Many times**: 2 points

----

13. I've taken, posted, or forwarded an embarrassing picture or video of someone else.

☐ **Never**: 0 points   ☐ **Once or twice**: 1 point   ☐ **Many times**: 2 points

14. I've gone off on someone multiple times while online gaming because they irritated me or said or did something stupid in the game.

☐ **Never**: 0 points   ☐ **Once or twice**: 1 point   ☐ **Many times**: 2 points

15. I've added mean, cruel, or embarrassing hashtags to social media posts.

☐ **Never**: 0 points   ☐ **Once or twice**: 1 point   ☐ **Many times**: 2 points

Total:

SCORING

0 points: Congratulations! It sounds like you treat people with respect and avoid participating in behaviors that could be viewed as cyberbullying. Keep up the good work—and encourage your friends and classmates to do the same.

1–15 points: You've contributed to the digital drama that makes life hard for some teens. You might not do it often, but it's still important for you to realize that some of what you're doing has been hurtful, or has encouraged others to be hurtful. Fortunately, you can use the information in this book to understand more about cyberbullying, and why it's a bad idea to take part in it—even if you *think* you're just joking around.

16–30 points: It sounds like you take part in cyberbullying behavior pretty often. You've probably wounded others badly with your words and actions. And on top of that, your behavior could have significant consequences for you, your reputation, your family, and your future. Make things right. Turn things around. Start doing what you know you should do—and help others change their attitudes and behaviors, too.

Start Standing Up, Not Standing By

I've seen kids who have been bullied, and I talk to them and sit by them. These kids were sad that they didn't have friends. They'd been called awful names for no reason. Now some of those kids are like brothers and sisters to me. I used to bully people, too. But now I've decided to say sorry for what I did wrong. I stopped bullying, and I stop other people from bullying. You gotta be there for kids who have been bullied. Step up and tell someone.

—Sean, 14, Oklahoma

We know from talking with teens that most haven't been cyberbullied personally—but most *have* seen it happening. We're willing to bet you've seen it, whether through a text, on social media, or elsewhere. And we also bet you'll see it again—probably in the near future. That's a problem, but it also means that there are plenty of chances for you to do your part in fighting against cyberbullying. You're not alone in this fight, and adults can help. But you know a lot more about what's going on online—both the good and the bad—than many adults do. And that means that you're in the best position to do something about the bad stuff.

> "If you are neutral in situations of injustice, you have chosen the side of the oppressor. If an elephant has its foot on the tail of a mouse, and you say that you are neutral, the mouse will not appreciate your neutrality."
> —Desmond Tutu

So what *do* you do when you see cyberbullying? For a lot of people, it depends partly on who's being targeted and who's doing the bullying. What if it's happening to one of your good friends? Do you act differently than if it's happening to the new kid at school, or a complete stranger?

> DOING NOTHING ACTUALLY *IS* DOING SOMETHING: IT'S SILENTLY AGREEING WITH THE BULLYING.

Maybe you're someone who always steps up, no matter what. Or maybe you tend to ignore stuff like that and dismiss it as drama that you don't want to get involved in. Maybe you think there's nothing you can do—that whatever you try won't really make a difference.

But you *can* make a difference, by becoming an "upstander." Stop standing by and start standing up for others. If you see bullying online—whether it's targeting a friend or a stranger—do something positive about it. Because doing nothing actually *is* doing something—something *negative*. It's silently agreeing with the bullying, and basically saying that it's okay with you—that it's not a problem. But if it's really not okay with you, let your actions reflect how you feel. Don't tolerate cruelty. Don't just accept hate. And if you're not sure exactly what to do, don't worry. That's where we come in! This chapter will give you practical suggestions and steps you can take to help people who are being cyberbullied, and to take a stand for what you know is right.

Standing up for others takes a lot of courage. But it's worth it. Think about what you really believe in and care about. What are your beliefs about right and wrong? What would you do if you saw other kinds of cruelty? For example, what would you do if someone was hurting your best friend, or your younger sister? Would you intervene? Or what if you saw an animal being mistreated? Would you step in, or call someone to help? These scenarios don't sound much like cyberbullying, but if you would help in these situations, why act any differently online? Cruelty is cruelty, and it should never be ignored.

> *I think the initial thought anyone would have about being a bystander to bullying is* "I would never do that—I would never just stand by!" *But once reality hits, this perception can change drastically. It's so much more convenient to ignore bullying, turn a blind eye, and pretend to overlook a problem that people think isn't their issue.*
>
> *Cyberbullying succeeds because it's easy to create this distance, this wall of separation. It's easy to assume that someone else will resolve a cyberbullying incident—that there are other people who will take action, so you don't have to.*
>
> *We all know what we should do if we see cyberbullying, but we don't always know if we would go out of our way to help someone we don't know very well. Helping a friend is one thing, but a stranger in need doesn't elicit the same sense of responsibility or loyalty. I really hope I'm someone who steps up to lend a hand when I witness cyberbullying, no matter who it is, instead of just staying silent. I know it's the right thing. And I know it's up to me to do it.*
>
> —Phelan, 16, New Jersey

Be There

The simplest thing that you can do when you see someone being treated badly is to be a friend to him. The moment when somebody's being harassed, teased, threatened, or humiliated is probably the very moment when he feels most alone. That person needs a reminder that others really do care. This knowledge won't make the pain of bullying disappear. But it *can* help someone get through a really hard time. And the sooner you step in, the better. We hear again and again that the longer cyberbullying goes on, the more it hurts—not just because of the bullying itself, but because it's so easy to dwell on what happened, replaying it over and over—and also worrying about what might happen next. By sticking up for someone in this situation, you can offer encouragement and help calm his or her fears.

So what does it mean to be there for someone? For one, it means paying attention. If you notice a person who seems to be struggling, ask if everything's okay. Let him know that you're available and willing to talk—or just listen. He may not open up to you at first.

But being there also means being persistent when it comes to caring about others. Keep checking in every now and then to remind him that you're there to help. You could also ask him if there's an adult at school that the person is close to, and if he'd mind if you told that adult what's going on.

You can also support people who are being bullied in many other small but meaningful ways. Send them friendly texts to make them feel better. Leave complimentary comments on their Instagram photos. Tweet them something sweet. Just be there for them. Because a lot of times, the bullying itself isn't even

Think About It

Q: Describe a recent cyberbullying incident that you saw. What happened? What did you do? What did others do? Later, did you feel like you could have or should have done more? Why or why not?

Q: Why do you think people are afraid to step up and do something when they see cyberbullying happening? What do you think could give more people the courage to be upstanders?

Respect Boundaries

When you're supporting someone who's being cyberbullied, your actions don't have to be big or loud—and sometimes, they shouldn't be. Especially if you don't know the person very well, be aware of how he or she seems to respond to attention and social situations. Some people are naturally quiet, shy, or self-conscious. They might not be comfortable with certain ways of showing encouragement. Others are very private and won't want everyone to know their business or what they're going through. Use your judgment and respect other people's boundaries, especially when they're different from your own. That's a way of showing support, too.

the worst part of a cyberbullying situation. Instead, it's the feelings of loneliness, rejection, and being singled out for hate and ridicule that do the most damage. But one person can make a difference, by trying to help fight those feelings and fears. And in time, people will take notice of your actions. You might inspire them to stand up for others, too.

> "You don't forget the face of the person who was your last hope."
> —*Katniss Everdeen in* The Hunger Games *by Suzanne Collins*

Build a Group Effort

After stepping in and being a friend to someone who's being cyberbullied, think about taking your efforts even further. Consider getting some of your friends to come together and rally around that person. This can help you as well as the person you're supporting. After all, there is strength—and safety—in numbers. Even when you most want to do what's right, you'll probably still be at least a little worried about becoming the next target. But if your voice is echoed by others, you'll feel stronger and more secure.

Hopefully, it won't be too hard to gather support from people you know. But you can look further, too. Encourage the person you're standing up for to look for help online. The Internet can bring out the worst in people sometimes, but it can also be a source of real encouragement. Sarah, a 17-year-old senior from Florida, experienced this firsthand. She made a Facebook group to talk about the cyberbullying she'd been going through. At first she didn't get anyone at school to be on her side. But the Facebook page quickly went viral in her town. Before long, lots of people were sharing their feelings, opinions, and passionate anti-bullying messages on Sarah's page. In turn, that led to improvements at her school and in her community.

Not everyone who's being cyberbullied will be up for the challenge of sharing his or her story online. It requires putting yourself out there, and when you're already feeling vulnerable, that can seem downright scary. You and others can take courage and comfort, though, in knowing that most people—at your school, in your town, and around the world—want to end bullying and cyberbullying. If you reach out, you might be surprised by how many people are willing to help.

Crush Cruel Content

We've all seen it happen—the hilarious YouTube video, funny meme on Tumblr or High School Memes, or awesome Instagram picture that goes viral in an instant. One moment that cat video only has a handful of views, and the next time you check, it's up to a few thousand—or a few million! In the same way, online rumors, gossip, and other hurtful content can go from person to person to person in just seconds. This leads not only to more people—maybe *a lot* more—seeing the mean or embarrassing post or photo, but also to greater pain because of the cruel things that might be posted in response.

This chain reaction can be devastating. But you can help stop it in its tracks by never forwarding or sharing cruel or inappropriate content. When you do face these situations—moments when you have to decide whether to participate, step aside, or speak up—how will you respond? That will come down to whether you have the courage to stand up for what's right. If you watch a video and see that the comment thread underneath is filled with insults, are you willing to step up and tell everyone to cut it out? Or if you see an embarrassing picture being retweeted over and over again, will you try to end the humiliation by sending modified tweets (MTs) or direct messages (DMs) telling others to stop the drama? You may be part of a group text that keeps making fun of a girl who made a simple mistake. Do you have the guts to tell everyone to let it go? Do *something*—something positive. Be part of the solution.

During my sophomore year, I was first bullied and then cyberbullied. At the beginning of the year, I mainly hung out with two friends. By midyear I'd distanced myself from them since they would leave me out of things constantly. One day I decided to just stop talking to them. After that, one of the girls thought it was funny to physically bump into me every time she saw me in school, no matter where I was or who I was with. At first I didn't say or do anything. I thought it was really dumb and I figured eventually she would stop. But one day I finally confronted her and told her to quit. She just laughed and continued pushing me. And again I continued ignoring her.

Then one day after school I was away with my team at a game. These girls who were bullying me had gone around asking people to fill a cup with urine. Some people did it with no idea what it was for. The girls themselves filled cups, too. Then they dumped them all over my locker and my things. One day at lunch everyone was talking about what had been done to a locker. Right then I recognized the locker number and said it was mine.

One of my teammates told me that she was sorry, but that she couldn't tell me who did it. She said they'd told her they were going to do it, but she hadn't really thought they would. Throughout the day people came to me confessing and apologizing, but no one would tell me for sure who did it. I went to my dean's office and told him what had happened. He brought in the girls, who denied it. The next day I got Facebook messages from people saying the girls had done it. After that the school told me they'd suspend them, but then the suspension was only for one day.

Next the girls started writing very mean things about me on Facebook and formspring. After reading all the messages I was so upset that I had panic attacks and had to go to the hospital. My parents printed out all the messages that the girls had written, and with those messages and the hospital papers we went to the police station.

The sheriff called the girls and their parents for a meeting the next day along with me and my parents. The parents denied that their daughters had done anything. The police officer just gave the girls a warning and told me that they'd watch for any online messages involving me. But the messages continued. The police and the school didn't take action, and the girls went back to school like nothing had happened. Having all this happen to me made me unsure of people.

—Lia, 16, New Mexico

Talk to a Trusted Adult

In Lia's story, her parents supported her. But a lot of other adults let her down. So did classmates who had the chance to stick up for her but stood by instead. Even though not everyone was helpful, Lia did take the right steps by reaching out and asking for support—even though that can be hard. In fact, we hear over and over from teens that they're reluctant to tell adults about cyberbullying. Whether it's happening to them, their friends, or complete strangers, a lot of teens think that telling an adult what's going on will somehow end up making it *worse*. Frankly, we don't blame you for being cautious or skeptical. Like you—and like Lia—we've seen some adults handle these situations in ways that *do* make them worse. An unhelpful adult might dismiss the behavior as "not that big of a deal," or respond by taking away the phone or computer of the person being targeted—as if that makes sense or makes the issue go away. Other times, an unhelpful adult confronts the person who is bullying, or his or her parents, in a clumsy way that doesn't solve the problem at all, and might even make things harder for the person being cyberbullied.

All of these things are possible, unfortunately. That's why you need to talk to a *trusted* adult. This is someone who will listen carefully to you when you explain the problem, and will ask what *you* would like to see happen—someone who will make sure your voice is heard, and will work with you to come up with a plan that makes sense. This trusted adult can often work behind the scenes to resolve a bullying problem without directly or publicly involving you. And ideally, this adult is someone who is pretty savvy when it comes to technology and can help you decide what action you should take on your own to protect yourself today and to prevent future problems.

Naturally, some adults are going to be better than others at helping you stop the bullying. If you don't know who this is in your life, take the time to find out. That person could be:

Someone at school. Is there a teacher you feel close to? What about a counselor or the principal? Or, if your school has a resource officer, liaison officer, or other police officer who regularly visits your campus, she might be a good person to talk to. For one thing, the officer may have been assigned to your school partly because she cares a lot about helping students with conflicts involving their peers—including harassment and bullying. And if the officer has been around for a while, she has probably handled situations similar to yours before.

A coach, mentor, faith leader, or someone else in the community. If you belong to any clubs or teams, think about the adults involved in those activities. Are any of them people you'd feel comfortable confiding in?

An adult at another school. Maybe you've tried to confide in many adults at your school but just don't feel like they are taking your problem seriously enough. If you have a friend who attends a different school, ask if she knows an adult in her school who might be able to help you. That person might even know someone else at *your* school who you didn't think to ask.

Your mom, dad, or another family adult. Do you think one of your parents is helpful when it comes to this sort of thing, and do you feel like you can talk to him or her honestly about it? If not, what about an aunt, uncle, or other relative?

Or, if you were given this book by an adult, that person would be a good place to start!

There *are* adults in your life who can help—you just have to figure out who they are. And here's some good news: Times are changing. The topic of bullying is getting more and more attention from politicians, actors, musicians, and many other people in the spotlight. As a result, teachers, counselors, and other people at your school now know more than ever about how to help you with bullying. And most of them want to do whatever they can to break through whatever hesitation you (and your peers) might have about telling them what's going on. Give them the opportunity to come through for you.

Giving adults a chance to help means taking a chance of your own. But it's a good gamble to take. Don't let someone suffer in silence. Don't sit back and just hope that the problem will go away on its own. Because unfortunately, it probably won't. Meanwhile, that person will keep being wounded. So figure out which adult you feel comfortable talking to, and be honest with her. If you're nervous about her response—and even scared that it could make the situation worse—say so upfront. Then just lay out the facts. Trust that the person you've picked will hear you out and then

> "Bullying is not a rite of passage or harmless part of growing up. It's wrong. It's destructive and we can all prevent it."
> —*President Barack Obama*

carefully consider an appropriate response. And if the situation seems especially complicated, feel free to have her contact us at **help@wordswound.org**. We promise to respond with our advice and feedback. We're here to help!

Also, if you figure out who you can go to at your school, make sure you tell others. In particular, younger students or those who are new to your school might not know where to turn for help. So if you do find someone, don't keep that information to yourself! You could even tell your principal how much you admire and appreciate this person. That way, she can be recognized for being there for students. Hopefully that will motivate other adults at school to learn more about helping students with these issues.

We know that some teens *do* struggle with getting the adults in their life to listen. Don't give up. Keep working to find an adult who will help you. And if you see someone else being bullied, do what you can to help him. He might be feeling hopeless and alone—and you might be the person to change that.

Think About It

Q: Which adult (or adults) do you feel you can turn to when you see someone being cyberbullied? Is there anyone you definitely *wouldn't* want to tell? Why or why not?

Record It and Report It

Back in **Chapter 2**, we talked about why it's important to save the digital evidence if you're being cyberbullied. When you go to an adult for help (or when you contact a website or service provider), that evidence helps prove who did what and when. This evidence can also help if you see someone else being cyberbullied. Take screenshots of cruel, offensive, or harmful behavior that you notice online. Then you can send these images to the websites where they appeared. The easiest way to do this is to compose a message to the email address **abuse@[websitename].com**. For example, if you see cyberbullying on Twitter, you can send a screenshot of the problem (and any other information you want to provide, such as the address of the profile or feed) to **abuse@twitter.com**. If you see obscene or cruel comments on Instagram, you'd send the content to **abuse@instagram.com**. In addition, most sites have a "Help," "Safety," or "Contact" section with information on how to make a report. For an up-to-date list of some of these resources, check our website at **wordswound.org/report**.

Many people don't contact websites with evidence of cyberbullying because they're afraid that the person they're reporting will find out about it and retaliate. But a reputable site will never tell the person doing the bullying that you were the person who reported him. You'll remain anonymous, it will only take a few minutes, and you'll be helping keep the site free of words and images that could inflict a lot of pain.

You may also be able to help someone who's being harassed via text by encouraging him to block or ignore texts (and calls) from unknown or unwanted numbers. Every bit of advice or support you provide can help the person cope, respond, and feel better about the situation.

> *Somebody on Twitter bullied me every day for more than a month. She would threaten me, and tell me to go self-harm. She even* told me to commit suicide *on numerous occasions. She'd tell me I deserved to get stabbed 18x, shot 20x, and run over by a truck. She told my friends fake stuff about me, like saying I'd written tweets hating on my friends, which I never did. She threatened me to the point that people were telling me to call the police. The cyberbullying only stopped when I emailed Twitter to get her account deactivated. I was desperate and I didn't see any other choice at that moment. Whatever would stop her from attacking me, that's what I would do. Finally Twitter suspended her account.*
>
> —Heather, 18, Texas

After I was bullied and cyberbullied, I lost all my so-called friends. I am no longer happy with myself. If something like this happens to you, or if you see it, make sure to report it. Would you rather be called a "snitch," or be hurt—or let someone else be hurt? Think about it. Bullying is NOT okay. No matter how little it seems, report it.

—Mila, 16, California

Anonymous Reporting at School

Some schools have anonymous reporting systems to deal with bullying and cyberbullying among students. Find out if your school is one of them. Maybe the school website includes a form you can fill out to report bullying. Or maybe there's a number you can call or text with information. If your school does have a system like this, use it. Don't hesitate. If you know something is going down, and someone is being harmed, let the school know so they can investigate and address the issue.

You might be worried about others finding out that you spoke up, but try not to let that stop you. For one thing, your school *should* realize that they need your trust (and the trust of your classmates) if you're going to use the reporting system. They definitely shouldn't want to violate that trust.

So fill out that form, make that call, or send that text. Provide as much or as little information as you want. You're the school's eyes and ears in the halls and in cyberspace. Teachers and other staff need your help to prevent or end conflict, drama, or bullying—and to make sure a situation doesn't turn into something even worse.

If your school doesn't have an anonymous reporting system, talk to people about setting one up. Get input and support from trusted teachers, friends, the student council, and more. Then you can connect with the principal or other school officials to talk about your ideas. Share how much you think this kind of system would help students feel safe. You might end up helping your school make a huge change for the better.

> *As a bystander in a cyberbullying situation, you play a crucial role. I know it may be easier to ignore the situation. But instead, you have to acknowledge it and take action—both in an attempt to solve the current issue, and to prevent future situations from arising. Most of all, as a bystander, you need to support the person being bullied in his or her time of need.*
>
> —Kylie LeMay, 18, Colorado

Step Up, Speak Up, Stand Up

As we've said, it's almost a sure thing that you'll witness cyberbullying at some point—if you haven't already. And you'll probably see it quite a few times. In fact, we have yet to meet any teens who *haven't* seen cyberbullying in some way, shape, or form by the time they graduate from high school. That's why it's so important for bystanders to become upstanders. There are lots of

DON'T STAND BY.
DON'T STAY SILENT.

ways you can do this, from being a good friend to documenting and reporting what you see. Some options will be pretty easy, while others will definitely be harder and take more courage and strength. But they're all worth doing.

Still, people often hesitate to do anything. They tell themselves that they should mind their own business and just stay out of it. Or they hold back because they don't want to be the next person harassed, or because they don't want to be known as a "rat." Plus, sometimes it's hard to know exactly *what* to do. There are all kinds of reasons why we might see what's happening to those around us and decide to shrug it off.

But remember the stories you've heard and read about people who have been cyberbullied. Some wrestle with serious psychological and emotional problems. Some try to cope by hurting others or hurting themselves. Some even feel like there's no escape other than taking their own life. Now think about your friends, siblings, or anyone you care about struggling in this terrible way. Wouldn't you want someone to come to their rescue?

That's why you have to step up. Don't stand by. Don't stay silent. And don't regret *not* doing what you could to help someone who desperately needs it.

Think About It

Q: If you were being cyberbullied, what would you want someone who saw it to do? What would you *not* want a bystander to do? Why?

The first time I witnessed cyberbullying, I didn't quite know what to do. No matter how many times I'd heard about the topic, I still wasn't sure how to act when the time came. Then I put myself in the other person's shoes. I realized that if I were in his or her position, I would hope someone would tell a counselor. So that's what I did. I acted before things got any worse. It's a sad truth that even after all the assemblies and guest speakers, teens will still cyberbully. But hopefully, people will begin to take a stand like I did. Don't sit back and become a bystander—be an upstander!

—John, 16, New Jersey

Scenario 5
In the library
name and pa
in the row a
What would

_____

_____

_____

_____

_____

_____

_____

_____

Scenario (
While surf
about Mic
hurtful int
What wou

_____

_____

_____

_____

_____

_____

_____

_____

??? Status Update: What Would You Do?

Read the following scenarios and think about what you would do in each situation. Write down your ideas, or talk them over with someone else.

Scenario 1

Sam has been getting messages like "you're such a loser" and "you suck" from a couple of people at school. He deletes the messages, but they keep coming. He asks you for help.
What would you do?

_____

_____

_____

_____

_____

_____

Scenario 2

You and a few of your friends get a text from Blake. The text includes pictures of your classmate Emma wearing a bikini. The message labels her "a whale," and Blake tells you to forward the photos to all your friends.
What would you do?

_____

_____

_____

_____

_____

_____

_____

_____

Scenario 3
You're in the co
of you, upload
bullied.
What would yo

_____

_____

_____

_____

_____

_____

_____

Scenario 4
Your best fri
sure who m
tell it's reall
What would

_____

_____

_____

_____

_____

_____

_____

_____

Chapter 5

Stay Smart and Stay Safe

I use social media all the time, and so there's probably way too much about me out there for others to find. I Google my name every now and then but there's gotta be more I can do to keep tabs on it all, right?

—Wyatt, 15, Montana

12 Tips for Protecting Yourself

If you've been cyberbullied, maybe you wonder if there was anything you could have done to keep it from happening—or anything you could do to keep it from happening in the future. Being cyberbullied is *never* your fault. But you *can* take steps to protect yourself. In this chapter, we give you **12 practical strategies** that can help reduce the chances that you'll be cyberbullied. All of these tips are related to the overall idea of

"I don't believe society understands what happens when everything is available, knowable, and recorded by everyone all the time."
—*Eric Schmidt, Google*

thinking carefully and acting wisely regarding what you share with others and who you interact with online. You probably won't be able to prevent every single instance of harassment or mistreatment, but these suggestions will definitely reduce the likelihood of it happening.

1. Be Careful with Content

The next time you text, tweet, email, or post, take a minute to think about the fact that any*thing* you do online could eventually be seen by any*one*. Even though you may think that only certain people can see your content, you never really know for sure. Once a piece of information enters cyberspace, you lose control over it. If you take a picture of yourself and send it to someone or post it on your Tumblr feed or Facebook profile, you no longer have complete control over what happens to that picture. It might end up on your principal's desk, in the hands of a police officer, or even on the front page of your local newspaper. (Or we might end up using your post in one of our presentations—in front of thousands of your fellow teens—as an example of "what NOT to do"!)

If content does get into the wrong hands, it can have consequences that you never expected. You may have heard about embarrassing or incriminating pictures and videos that prevented teens from winning scholarships, getting into their chosen universities, or landing their dream jobs. You also probably know that there could be somebody out there who envies you or has a problem with you for some reason. That person might decide to use those pictures and videos (or any other content you share online) to make you look bad, make your life miserable, or both.

Obviously, you don't want to live in fear that every post or picture could lead to some sort of chain reaction that ruins your entire future. We don't want you to live that way, either. But it *is* smart to be thoughtful about what you put out there. Trust your gut, exercise wisdom, and learn about the various ways you can protect yourself.

2. The Internet Never Forgets

In addition to being seen by more people than you expect, what you post online may also be out there for much *longer* than you expect. This can be a good thing sometimes. Part of the reason we record our thoughts, pictures, and experiences is so we can remember and relive those moments later. But it can be really bad when something silly or embarrassing you post today sticks around for years and years. When you put something online, think about how you'd feel if your parents, future college admissions officer, or prospective boss saw it. Even if you're savvy enough to limit who can see your social media posts, you can't know for sure who might save them on their computers or phones, forward them to others, modify or doctor them in some way, and repost them, or print them out to pass around.

In addition, questionable pictures or other content that's tagged with your name (or linked to you in some other way) can cast you in a negative light, regardless of who put the content online in the first place. For example, a friend might tag you as part of a crude meme or joke on Facebook. Then others might see the post as representing exactly what you think or feel—whether that's true or not. If something like this happens, the first step you should take is to untag yourself. You can also adjust your privacy settings so that no one can tag you without your approval. Even if the picture or post represents something perfectly legal, justified, or just an inside joke, you never know how an outsider might view it. Others could perceive something in a way that makes you look immature, foolish, or ridiculous.

Whether you like it or not, some people *will* judge you based on how you appear online. That's just the way it is. And it can be almost impossible to completely remove something from the Internet once it's out there. So do your best not to let anything be posted that is likely to compromise your reputation or be used against you. Be sure that your friends know where you stand when it comes to what's being said about you on social media. Talk with them about the issue so that they'll be less likely to post anything about you (or themselves) that could be problematic. Also, *keep* making sure that everyone's on the same page, because people may forget if you just bring up the subject once. Your friends need to know how important your digital reputation is to you. And hopefully they'll start thinking about their own in the same way.

3. Google Yourself

One smart way to protect yourself from cyberbullying and related online dangers is to keep an eye on what has been said or posted about you. You can do this by regularly using Google, Bing, Yahoo, or other popular search engines to look for your full name and the screen names you use on social media sites. The more sites you use to search, the better, because each one might lead you to different material. If you have a fairly unusual first and last name, that's probably all you'll need to search for. People with more common names (like James Smith) may need to include a city or school name to narrow the search. Maybe *you* rarely or never post anything that you're worried about. But what if someone *else* does? Any personal information (like your birth date, address, or phone number), photos, videos, or other content that comes up when searching for your full name or your screen names could be a potential problem. A person who is cyberbullying you—or intends to—can easily use this information against you.

Say, for example, someone really doesn't like you. She searches online and finds a photo of you in your swimsuit at the pool. Then she notices that you've posted your cell phone number in a comment on a status update. She could use a meme generator to add text to the photo saying, "For a good time, call [your phone number]." Then she might post that captioned photo all over Instagram with hashtags like #whore, #slut, and a hashtag associated with your high school (so lots of your classmates notice it). This entire situation could have been avoided if she hadn't been able to see your pictures, and if you hadn't posted your phone number publicly.

The sooner you spot content about you that shouldn't be widely visible, the sooner you'll be able to get it removed. To do this, you can contact the site through their **abuse@** email address (see pages 94–95), and ask them to pull it down because of cyberbullying concerns. There are also companies that—for a fee—will do the work of contacting various sites across the Internet to have unflattering or undesirable content of yours deleted. (These companies might also intentionally post a lot of positive content about you in order to push the negative stuff farther down the list of search engine results). But you can do most of this by yourself.

KEEP AN EYE ON WHAT HAS BEEN SAID OR POSTED ABOUT YOU.

In addition to Google and other general search engines, it is important to check out people-search sites that collect personal information about Internet users, such as **zabasearch.com, spokeo.com, pipl.com,** and **peekyou.com.** You may be shocked by how much you find about yourself on these sites, such as your age, current address, previous addresses, phone numbers, and names of relatives. You can also use the Wayback Machine on **archive.org** to view what a website looked like at a specific date in the past by entering the URL you'd like to check out. This could be useful if someone posted something about you but then removed it before you had a chance to save a copy as evidence. Not all pages are archived on this site (many social networking profiles are not), but it's definitely worth a look.

4. Keep Tabs on Your Digital Reputation

Apart from typing your name into search engines every so often to see what shows up, there are other online tools that can help you stay on top of your digital reputation. One easy way to stay in tune with what's said about you online is to sign up for Google Alerts (**google.com/alerts**). Set up an alert using your first and last name (and any other keyword or phrase you want, such as the screen names you use, or your high school's name). Then you'll get emails from Google when these keywords show up in any article or story. For example, if James Smith from Hoyt Lakes, Minnesota, wants to keep track of what's being said about him, he could set up a Google Alert with the keywords "James Smith" and "Hoyt Lakes." Anytime Google's search robot finds those phrases together, James will get an email letting him know about it. (By the way, you can also use this technique to stay informed on cyberbullying issues by subscribing to a Google Alert using the keyword "cyberbullying." It's that simple!)

Another popular tool is **socialmention.com**. This site monitors more than 100 social media sites and lets you perform keyword searches of the results. Just as you can on Google, you can set up email alerts on Social Mention to let you know whenever your name (or any keyword you choose) pops up on social media. A similar tool is called **nutshellmail.com**. It also works by sending you email updates. Something especially cool about this site, though, is that it keeps you informed about mentions, tweets, news-feed updates, tagging, messages, friends, and followers on Facebook, Twitter, YouTube, and other sites. Anything that involves you, your name, your profile, or your feed is identified, compiled, and then sent to you in an email. Basically, Google Alerts and other search engines help you stay up to date with what's said *about* you anywhere online, while Social Mention and Nutshell Mail help you keep tabs on what's being said about you and also *to* you, with a focus on the social side of the Web.

> **Think About It**
>
> **Q:** Go to Google and search for your name and hometown. What comes up? Try this again on another site like Social Mention. Is there anything in the results that worries you? If so, what suggestions from this chapter can you use to address those worries and to prevent them from cropping up in the future?

5. Never Respond to Mysterious Messages

Would you mail a letter in response to a piece of physical junk mail that showed up at your home? Probably not—partly because that would be a little weird, but also because it would be a pain. As a matter of fact, you probably don't even read most junk mail. In the case of email, though, it's a lot easier to click that new message in your inbox and open something that turns out be spam—or worse. And it's also a lot easier to write back. But it's usually not a good idea to respond to messages—whether they're emails, texts, Facebook messages, direct messages on Twitter, or other kinds of messages—from anybody you don't know. You might not even want to open and read those messages. If you do, be sure not to click on any links or attachments they contain. These might include or lead to viruses that can infect your computer or phone—possibly without you knowing it right away. A virus could then cause serious damage. It might delete or corrupt all of your data. Or the virus might install a harmful program called a Trojan horse, which collects your personal or private information. Whoever sent the message can then use that information to steal your identity, spam all your contacts, and cause all sorts of other trouble.

> *When I was checking my email one day, I opened up my inbox and there was a person who was incredibly mad at me. Why? I don't know. I didn't recognize the username so I just deleted the messages and moved on. But this person emailed me again and again, sending similar messages over and over. I deleted all of them and logged off. The next day the same person was emailing me, calling me names, and telling me to die because no one would care, saying I would never get a girlfriend, etc. But then the very next day, they said they loved me and were sorry! I was so confused. I told the person I wasn't whoever they thought I was, and they sent me an email filled with cussing and death threats, then taking it back with "LOL JK!" Finally I blocked them. I don't know why I didn't do it sooner.*

—Oskar, 14, Illinois

6. Always Log Out

Many social media sites like Facebook, Twitter, and Instagram let you remain logged in even after you close your Web browser or switch out of the app on your phone. This feature is convenient when you revisit the site, because you don't have to reenter your username and password. The problem is that anyone else who uses your device can also easily access your account if your log-in credentials are stored in the system. Here's one scenario we hear about a lot—think about whether it's ever happened to you: You've been checking Facebook on your family's computer, and then you leave without logging out. Your mom uses the computer next, and she surfs over to Facebook. While she's there she clicks "Like" on the fan page for her favorite TV show, sends a friend request to her coworker, and comments on your brother's latest post. Unfortunately, she does all of this while logged into *your* account!

While this is a relatively harmless mistake that's easy to clear up, what if the next person on that computer were someone who felt like hurting you? Maybe you forget to log out of Twitter after using a computer at the school library, and the next student who sits down is someone who wants to mess with you. He or she might take advantage of the opportunity and post something hurtful or humiliating.

Luckily, it's really easy to prevent this sort of thing. Always completely log out after using *any* social media site, webmail program, or similar account. This is especially important if you're using a public computer, but it's best just to be in the habit of signing out, even on your own phone or laptop.

7. Protect Your Password

Think about how many times *every day* you use a password on a phone, computer, social media site, or another online account. Passwords are a huge part of our daily lives. Technically, they serve as authentication to identify people as being who they claim to be. Correct authentication is supposed to prevent others from accessing or altering your personal data, so passwords should be kept very secure. Unfortunately, some people put themselves at risk of cyberbullying, identity theft, or other dangers by sharing or exposing their passwords. For instance, we've asked hundreds of groups of students if they know any of their friends' passwords. More than half of them always say yes!

> *I'd chosen to give my Facebook password to one of my "best friends." She was friends with a girl who I'd been having some bullying problems with. One day my "friend" was at my enemy's house and decided to get on my Facebook and delete all my pictures. Then they took a picture of this boy that I really liked and put it as my profile picture. They wrote "I miss you," "I'm in love with you," "I cry about you all the time," all over my profile so all my friends saw it. It was really stupid, but it hurt me so badly.*
>
> —Mei, 15, North Carolina

Maybe you would never share your passwords on purpose. But you still might reveal them accidentally. A lot of people store and remember their passwords in ways that make it easy for others to find them. One person might leave her passwords on a sticky note next to her computer, or taped under her keyboard. Someone else might save them in a text file right on his computer's desktop. Another person might even leave them in a small notebook that she carries around in her backpack or purse, or in the Notes app on her phone. It doesn't take Sherlock Holmes to notice these sorts of things!

Even if you're careful about never putting your passwords in easy-to-find places, and even if you never share them with others, that doesn't mean they're completely safe. For example, some websites have security questions that let users retrieve forgotten passwords. If the user answers the questions correctly, he gets an email with a link to reset the password. Common password hint questions include "What is your pet's name?" or "What is your mother's maiden name?" If someone knows the answers to these questions and can also get into your email account, he might be able to access a lot of your other information, too. And *that* might allow him to change passwords on your other online accounts—simply by having access to your email and knowing a few basic facts about you.

Some people use the same password for multiple accounts—school and personal email, Facebook, Twitter, Instagram, Skype, eBay, PayPal, and more. That makes it easy to remember, but it also means that if someone finds out the password to a single account, he can then get into all the other ones, too. So it's wise to have a different password for every site or account you use, and to keep track of all your passwords in a way that's safe and secure, yet still convenient.

For example, some people use built-in password managers in Web browsers. Others use a secure online service like Clipperz, which encrypts all of your passwords so that even the people behind the site can't decipher them. Other people use free software such as KeePass, which keeps all of your passwords in a secure database and requires you only to remember one master password to access them.

You could also choose a lower-tech method, such as:

1. Create a long numbered list of 30 (or more) passwords. Some might not be ones you're actively using.

2. Save this list as a file on your computer. Give the file a nonobvious name and stash it in a nonobvious file folder.

3. On a sheet of paper, write a list of websites where you have accounts. Number the list. Each number represents which password on the computerized list goes with that site.

4. Hide this sheet of paper somewhere in your room or elsewhere at home.

Tools for Building a Super-Strong Password

- Make your password at least seven characters long

- Use a mixture of numbers, UPPER- and lowercase letters, and nonalphabetic characters (&%$@)

- Use the first letters of a sentence, song lyric, poem, movie quote, or other text. For example, "like the Ceiling can't hold Us" becomes "ltCchU"

- Use made-up words not found in the dictionary (mihtaupyn)—as long as you can remember them!

- Use short words separated by nonalphabetic characters (dog%door; candy$corn)

- Use transliteration or leetspeak, using numerals in place of some letters (for example, "EliteOne" becomes "El1te0n3")

- Jumble up the letters in two words: ("Play Date" becomes "PateDlay")

Whatever method you use to keep track of your passwords, take the time to figure out a solution that doesn't leave you vulnerable to cyberbullying or other online risk.

In addition to all these precautions, don't forget to change your password regularly. No matter how unusual and hard to guess, your password could be compromised without you even knowing it. Sometimes hackers access passwords by finding security holes in databases for popular websites and online stores. Once a hacker or a cyberbully has gotten to your password, he might also be able to find your name, email address, and other personal information which could then be used to steal your identity. Sometimes the companies or websites themselves don't even know that the information has been stolen until weeks or months later. So it's best to change your password at least once a year. Pick a time of year that will remind you to make the switch. Get in the habit of changing your passwords at the start of each school year, on your birthday, or on some other memorable date. Just make sure you don't let passwords get stale!

8. Guard Your Goods

It's almost as important to protect your phone, laptop, and other digital gadgets you might have as it is to protect your passwords. We hear a lot of stories about phones and iPads being pulled out of backpacks, desks, and even back pockets. Usually whoever does this is just joking around, but sometimes it can get serious. If someone gets into your phone, for example, she could impersonate you and prank call your friends, post or tweet embarrassing stuff, or text your crush revealing your personal feelings. Someone could also bully or threaten others using your phone, leading them to report you to adults or to retaliate against you. Again, somebody

Sneaking Past the Gate

If you have an iPhone, make sure that someone can't bypass the passcode and use Siri by holding down the home button and telling her to do something sketchy (like update Twitter or Facebook with an offensive post). Many people don't realize that you can still use Siri this way, even with a passcode in place, unless you make a specific change on your phone. To do this, go into the Settings on your phone, and tap the General section. Find the Passcode Lock setting, and the option to Allow Access When Locked: Siri. Finally, make sure the toggle is set to OFF!

might just do these things because she thinks it's funny. But it's not a laughing matter at all when you're left to deal with the fallout.

The best way to prevent this scenario is also the simplest: Don't let others get ahold of your stuff. Don't leave your phone on the table in the cafeteria when you go throw your trash away. Don't leave your laptop open when your brother's or sister's friends could use it without you knowing. Take a few minutes to lock down *all* of your devices with passcodes (or secret swipe patterns on some phones). This might sound like a pain, but it could save you a lot of time, hassle, and heartache in the long run.

9. Be Picky About Your Privacy

You probably feel like you're *always* hearing about how you really need to lock down the privacy settings for your online accounts. You probably also know that this is the best way to protect not only your profile as a whole, but also individual pieces of content. The trouble is that a lot of people never get around to doing these things. Or, if they do, they don't revisit the settings as often as they should—even though websites frequently make changes and tweaks that affect who can contact them and who sees what they share.

Yes, it's a chore to maintain all these settings. Yes, it's easy to procrastinate and tell yourself that you'll do it next time. We've talked to many teens who say just that—they tell us that they totally *meant* to set up all the right blocks and restrictions, but they were just too busy, or didn't think they'd ever actually deal with a privacy issue or bullying problem on social media. Unfortunately, many of them were wrong, and ended up with serious regrets. It's a lot like when you keep reminding yourself to back up your data on your computer, but keep putting it off. Then your hard drive crashes and you lose all your photos, all your music, and more. It's a pretty awful feeling.

Don't let that be the case when it comes to protecting your privacy online, and don't put it off any longer. Take the time *today* to protect yourself on Instagram, Twitter, Facebook, Tumblr, YouTube, and any other sites you use. Each social media platform gives you the tools and options to safeguard what you share, and with whom you share it. It just takes a few minutes of looking in the right places, and making the right changes.

If you aren't sure how to manage these settings, start by searching for a privacy or safety center on whichever site you're using. For example, Facebook has a Safety Center (at **facebook .com/safety**) where you can find tips on safe and responsible online social networking. You can also use Google and search phrases like "Instagram privacy settings" or "Twitter block person," or you can check out YouTube for some how-to videos (there are lots!). You can also ask your friends or an adult who might know. Just know that there's *always* a way to control your information. After you figure out what to do, check to make sure you've done it right. To check just how visible your profile or account is, try to access your account, while not logged in, from a computer or device you've never used to log in. Type your name in the search box on the site and see what shows up, or search on Google using keywords such as your name or screen name. This will give you the perspective of someone who's trying to find information about you, but who isn't your friend. You may be surprised how much people can see about you without actually being connected to you on social media.

10. Location, Location, Location

Have you ever tweeted, snapped a pic, or posted a status update that included your location? The trend of location-based social networking allows people to use their smartphones to check in at various locations. Maybe you've done this with Twitter, Instagram, or Facebook to let friends know that you're on vacation, or at a local restaurant or concert. Some apps, like Foursquare, scan for where you are and identify what's around you. The app then gives you points, badges, and titles (such as Mayor or Superuser), tips from other users, and special deals. For example, a girl could use Foursquare to check in at her local Starbucks. When she does, she might get a coupon on her phone to use on her next coffee purchase at the café.

At first glance, location sharing may not seem like a big deal. In fact, it might seem like a really *good* deal, since it can get you bargains and discounts on products or services that you're buying anyhow, and clue you in to friends who are nearby. But the problem is when the site or app broadcasts your whereabouts for any and all to see. You may *want* your close friends to see where you are, so you can meet up and hang out. However, the app may also share this info with many other people and allow them to find you, too. That may sound harmless, but the unfortunate fact is that you're more

Please Rob Me!

A few years ago, a website called **pleaserobme.com** got a lot of attention. The site identified and gathered location-based posts from Foursquare and Twitter, and shared where people were at the moment based on searches by city and state. In particular, it revealed when they had checked in at locations away from their homes—potentially valuable information for would-be robbers.

The site's three founders didn't actually want people to get robbed. Instead, they wanted to show online users just how much information they were sharing, and how it might be used against them. But just because this site didn't have malicious intentions, that doesn't mean there aren't others out there that *do*. So don't take your safety for granted.

likely to be hurt or bullied by people who are already part of your life, rather than random strangers. So when you post information like your location online, someone you know might exploit the situation and use that information against you.

Let's say that the girl who checked in at Starbucks shared that check-in with all of her Twitter followers. Eventually her ex-boyfriend—who's still angry and hurt about the breakup—sees the tweet. He could decide to show up and yell at her, embarrass her in front of everybody at the coffee shop, or even do something more serious. This scenario might sound far-fetched, but there *have* been cases in which people who shared their locations were harassed or physically hurt.

In addition to actively checking in or sharing your location using Foursquare or similar apps, you might be sharing information without completely realizing it. Most smartphones, digital cameras, tablets, and similar devices include geotagging features. Geotagging ties location-based metadata into photos, videos, text messages, and other content. Metadata can contain a lot of information, such as precisely when and where a piece of content was created. (Remember the story of the Burger King employee on pages 75–76?)

This feature can be great if you're trying to remember exactly what beach you were on when you took that awesome sunset photo years ago. However, a picture of your girlfriend in her backyard may also contain the exact location of her house—and that's *not* so great.

Overall, the negatives of geotagging outweigh the positives. So before using a phone, camera, or tablet that might have the feature turned on (it's often enabled by default), think about whether it's worth the risk. If you decide it isn't, take a minute or two to disable the feature. After all, if you want others to know where you are— so they can meet up for a party, study session, coffee, or day at the park—you can always text or direct message them. This keeps uninvited guests from showing up.

11. Think Before You Friend or Follow

On top of setting up privacy protections on Facebook and other sites so that only your friends can see your posts and other information, it's also really important to know exactly *who* those friends are, and to make sure they're trustworthy. Sites like Twitter, Facebook, and Instagram are great for keeping in touch with friends and family members—especially those who live far away. But some people get caught up in a desire to rack up as many friends as they possibly can. The more connections you have online, some people think, the cooler, more popular, or more powerful you are. Plus, it just feels good to see the number of followers you have on Twitter or Instagram grow. But let's say you meet someone at a party or while playing a game online. The next thing you know, you're connected online. But how much do you *really* know about this new "friend"? In general, if you use common sense about what you post, there probably isn't a whole lot of risk. But you still don't want to reveal too much to a person until you're sure you can trust him.

THINK CAREFULLY ABOUT WHO YOU LET INTO YOUR ONLINE LIFE.

A school resource officer recently told us a story that showed how accepting unknown people as friends online can lead to trouble. Some seniors at the school had gotten Facebook friend requests from a man they didn't know. He told the students that he'd graduated from their school a few years ago and had just moved back to town. Now he wanted to reconnect with the community and the school. Based on this story, a few seniors decided it would be fine to friend him. The stranger then asked to be friends with many other students. Most were skeptical at first. But some did what many of us would do: They checked to see if they had any mutual friends with this person. When they noticed that a few seniors were friends with the guy, they thought he must be okay. Soon the man had friended many of the high school's students.

One day, the resource officer overheard some upperclassmen talking at lunch. They were saying that, despite a lot of them being Facebook friends with this guy, nobody actually knew who he was. When the officer investigated further, she found out that many of the students in the high school were friends with the stranger. She also learned that many middle schoolers and even some elementary-age students were friends with him, too. Like the seniors, they had seen a lot of familiar faces on his friends list, so they figured they didn't need to worry. But nothing could have been further from the truth. The resource officer learned that this stranger was actually abusing several of the elementary-school students.

When the seniors found out about this, they felt horrible. They thought that if they hadn't friended the guy in the first place, this whole thing wouldn't have happened. There's no way to know for sure whether that's true. The man may have simply found another way to exploit the kids at school. But either way, this story shows that who you friend is a reflection on you. If you're friends with someone on Facebook, you're basically saying that you believe the person can be trusted. If you *don't* trust the person enough to vouch for them to the rest of your friends, don't include them in your social network. Look over your list of friends and followers on the social media sites you use most. Do you really trust all of them fully? To protect yourself and your *real* friends, play it safe.

12. Catfishing

Obviously, connecting online with people you don't know in person can have unexpected dangers. One very specific risk is the chance that someone might be trying to mess with your heart by "catfishing." The Urban Dictionary defines a catfish as *"someone who pretends to be someone they're not using Facebook or other social media to create false identities, particularly to pursue deceptive online romances."*

You might have heard about catfishing in the 2010 documentary film or the 2012 MTV show, both titled *Catfish*. But you might not realize how catfishing can be tied to cyberbullying. The story of Megan Meier shows that catfishing does have connections to cyberbullying, that it can happen to anyone, and that it can have tragic consequences.

In 2006, when Megan was 13 years old, she began an online relationship with a boy she knew as Josh Evans. For almost a month, Megan corresponded with this boy exclusively online, because he said that he was homeschooled and that he didn't have a phone. One day in October of that year, Megan got a message from Josh saying, *"I don't know if I want to be friends with you any longer because I hear you're not nice to your friends."* This was followed by messages from other people calling Megan "fat" and a "slut," and one from Josh saying that the world would be better without her in it. These messages, along with other painful experiences in her life, were too much for Megan. She ran up to her room. A few minutes later, Megan's mother, Tina, went to check on her, and found her daughter hanging in her bedroom closet. Tina rushed Megan to the hospital, but it was too late. Megan died the next day.

After their daughter's death, the Meier family learned that the "boy" Megan had been corresponding with never existed. "Josh Evans" and his online profile were created by Lori Drew, the mother of a former friend of Megan's. Lori had made the profile as a way to spy on what Megan was saying about her daughter.

Another extreme example of catfishing is the case of Anthony Stancl. In 2009, Anthony was a high school senior in Wisconsin. He posed on Facebook as two girls named Kayla and Emily. One of them was totally made up and the other one was a real student at school. As Kayla and Emily, Anthony formed romantic relationships online with a number of boys at his high school. He then convinced at least 31 of those boys to send nude pictures or videos of themselves to "Kayla" and "Emily." Next, Anthony—still posing as the girls and still communicating through Facebook— tried to convince more than half of the boys to meet up with a male friend of the girls for sexual activities. The "girls" told the boys that if they refused, the nude pictures and videos would be shared for all to see. Seven boys said yes to the request. They met with the "male friend"—Anthony himself—and had sexual encounters with him. Anthony took pictures of these incidents with his phone. The police eventually found over 300 nude images of male teens on his computer. He was charged with several crimes including sexual assault and possession of child pornography, and in 2010 he received a 15-year prison sentence.

The cases of Megan Meier and Anthony Stancl are unusually serious. But milder incidents happen often. You might be thinking that there's no way in the world you'd ever fall prey to this kind of a scheme. But no one *really* thinks they'd ever be caught up in something like this. That's why it's so important to think carefully about who you let into your online life.

You might also think that people should know better than to start a relationship with someone they only know online. This is definitely a two-way street. It's never okay to use technology to fool someone. But it's also true that people need to be skeptical and cautious when entering into online relationships, and to realize that doing it at all will involve some risk. Those who do choose to have online romances should not limit their communication to

Think About It

Q: Do you think catfishing qualifies as cyberbullying? Why or why not? Why do you think people get caught up in catfishing schemes?

Q: Have you ever pretended to be someone you aren't online? If so, why? What happened?

Screen Names and Pseudonyms

Setting up a fake online profile to catfish is wrong. It also violates most social media sites' policies. For example, Facebook's Terms of Service state, in part: "You will not provide any false personal information on Facebook, or create an account for anyone other than yourself without permission."

But many people *do* use pseudonyms or alter-egos online. There are some perfectly good reasons for doing this, and as long as your actions under a pseudonym don't hurt anyone, it usually isn't a problem. It really comes down to your intention: Is it to protect yourself, or to hide while bullying others? It's one thing to be protective of your identity for privacy reasons, but it's another thing entirely to create an alternate identity so that you can humiliate or threaten someone else.

IMs, emails, and texts. They should also use Skype, FaceTime, or other video-chatting services that will let them see and interact in real-time with the people they're in touch with. If the other person keeps refusing to be seen in real life or online, that's a red flag. Plus, it's best not to give out too much personal information, especially early on. And if the time does come to meet, a person should *never* go alone to meet someone he or she knows only from cyberspace, but always go with a friend—or better yet, a group of friends. They can offer protection if something turns out to be not what it seems—and they can also provide an escape route if the meeting is more awkward and weird than awesome and wonderful.

Be Tech SMART

S: Stay safe by being suspicious. Not everyone is *really* your friend. Be somewhat skeptical at first about people you meet online. They might not be who they say they are. *Never* meet up alone with someone you only know online.

M: Manage your online information and your digital reputation. Don't put anything online you wouldn't want a lot of people to see or know (including personal information, racy pictures, and so on). Think about what someone would think of you judging solely by what's online. Could someone use what they find to harass, threaten, or blackmail you? Can others locate you from what you post online, and could they come find you if they really wanted to? Keep social networking profiles private and locked down, and don't let just anyone be your friend or follower. Be selective.

A: Act responsibly. Don't say anything to someone online that you wouldn't say to that person's face, or with your grandma, little brother, or favorite teacher in the room. Try not to joke around in a way that is likely to be misinterpreted or misunderstood by someone who doesn't know you very well.

R: Reach out to others. Be a mentor and a role model to other students, especially younger ones. Tell an adult if you see or hear about someone being mistreated (online or off). Don't stand by and let someone be bullied. If you see it happening and don't do something about it, you're participating along with the person actually doing the bullying.

T: Talk to adults about the technology you use. Teach them how to use your favorite social media sites. Show them what you like and don't like online. Gain their trust. The more you talk with adults about what's going on online, the more likely they are to trust you and to support you if you do run into trouble.

Take Control

You have a lot of power to control your online life and experiences. This means you can be smart and safe by taking some commonsense steps to protect yourself from cyberbullying and other dangers. Remember:

- Think carefully about what you share online.

- Take the time to set up proper, secure privacy settings and preferences on websites, software, and your devices.

- Report troubling status updates, captions, comments, posts, pictures, videos, notes, and tags to the websites where they appear.

- Don't feel obligated to respond to messages and friend requests that are annoying or threatening, or that come from people you don't know.

- Block certain people from communicating with you or reading some of the content you share. Only let those you know and trust into your online life.

- Turn off location-sharing and the ability to check in to places. If you need to let your friends know where you are, just text or call them rather than sharing it with your entire network of friends or followers.

Share these ideas and suggestions with your friends. Slowly but surely, you'll help make the Internet a safer, more respectful place to be.

Status Update: Are Your Social Media Habits Putting You At Risk?

Are you using social networking websites safely and responsibly? Answer these questions, add up your points, and then read about your score. Did you discover anything that surprised you? What will you do to change your habits and be safer online?

----

1. My Facebook privacy settings allow non-friends to see my pictures and/or other things on my profile.

☐ **No:** 0 points   ☐ **I'm not sure:** 1 point   ☐ **Yes:** 2 points

----

2. I've posted things online that I wouldn't want my parents to see.

☐ **Never:** 0 points   ☐ **Once or twice:** 1 point   ☐ **Many times:** 2 points

----

3. My friends don't set their social media accounts to be private.

☐ **No:** 0 points   ☐ **I'm not sure:** 1 point   ☐ **Yes:** 2 points

----

4. A friend knows my password for Instagram, Twitter, Facebook, or another social media site.

☐ **No:** 0 points   ☐ **I'm not sure:** 1 point   ☐ **Yes:** 2 points

----

5. When I search for my name on Google, my social media profiles show up in the results.

☐ **No:** 0 points   ☐ **I'm not sure:** 1 point   ☐ **Yes:** 2 points

----

6. I've posted my phone number on a social media site.

☐ **No:** 0 points   ☐ **I'm not sure:** 1 point   ☐ **Yes:** 2 points

----

7. I've posted something on social media about someone else that I wish I wouldn't have.

☐ **Never:** 0 points   ☐ **Once or twice:** 1 point   ☐ **Many times:** 2 points

----

---

8. An adult or friend has talked with me about a concern they had about something I posted online.

☐ **Never**: 0 points   ☐ **Once or twice**: 1 point   ☐ **Many times**: 2 points

---

9. I'm friends on Facebook with people I've never met in person.

☐ **No:** 0 points   ☐ **I'm not sure:** 1 point   ☐ **Yes:** 2 points

---

10. I've posted my school's name on a social media profile.

☐ **No:** 0 points   ☐ **I'm not sure:** 1 point   ☐ **Yes:** 2 points

Total:

SCORING

0 points: Congratulations! It looks like you're acting in safe and smart ways when it comes to social networking. You clearly take great care to protect your private information online, and that will help protect you from cyberbullies. Keep checking your privacy settings *regularly* to make sure everything's locked down.

1–10 points: You're acting pretty safely, but some of your online activity does put you at risk. Maybe you've posted a few photos that you shouldn't have, or you're not sure who can see what on your social media profiles. Take the time to get rid of questionable content and figure out those privacy settings. The good news is that it doesn't seem like you've put yourself out there too much, so you probably won't have too much trouble cleaning things up.

11–20 points: Your social media habits are definitely risky. But it's not too late to protect yourself and your privacy. Using the tips you're learning from this book, spend some time cleaning up your social media sites. Remove embarrassing pictures and videos, unfriend or unfollow people you don't know, and take control over who can see what you post online. The sooner you delete problematic content from your sites and profiles, the less likely it is that it might be used against you. So do it now!

Part Three

Building a Culture
of Kindness

Chapter 6

Delete Cyberbullying

Educators, administrators, and parents can preach against bullying all day, but it really hits home when your peers send the message. Students can relate and appeal to their fellow students much more than adults can.

—Danielle Soltren, 17, Florida

There's a great trend on the rise: More and more teens are taking stands (and taking action!) on issues that affect their lives and the lives of others. Some promote certain political views or candidates. Others spread messages about protecting the environment. Still others want to raise money and awareness to support causes or solve problems at home and around the world.

Maybe you're passionate about a cause and are already working to promote it. Or, maybe you haven't found an issue that really catches your attention yet, but reading this book has gotten you interested in doing something to end online harassment and hate. If you want to delete cyberbullying and spark change at your school, in your community, and beyond, this chapter will give you information on how to turn your ideas into action—today.

> "Unless someone like you cares a whole awful lot, Nothing is going to get better. It's not."
> —*Dr. Seuss*, The Lorax

You can get started on your own, or team up with a group of other teens who care. Maybe you'll start with one of these specific activities, or maybe you'll come up with new ideas. Why *not* you? Why *not* now?

Become an Expert

Cyberbullying is a tough and complex problem. There are so many details to consider in each case: Who's involved? How do they know each other? What sort of relationship do they have? Have there been problems between them in the past? Do their activities violate school policy or even break the law? Sometimes the news can make it seem like all cyberbullying incidents are the same: A mean kid is a jerk to a totally innocent kid who suffers as a result—and who may even feel driven to suicide. The truth is that every cyberbullying case is unique and complicated in its own way. And the misconceptions and lack of understanding that many people have about cyberbullying only make it harder to come up with real solutions. Fortunately, you can help correct these false assumptions and broaden people's understanding of cyberbullying.

Research the Problem

Become an expert on the topic of cyberbullying. Read as much as you can on the subject. This book is just a starting point. Check out **wordswound.org**, as well as reports from reliable news sources and research organizations (including our Cyberbullying Research Center at **cyberbullying.us**). Set up a Google Alert with the keyword "cyberbullying." Then share this information with others—using the ideas in this chapter, for example.

You can do a lot of research on your own. In addition, there are many caring and informed adults out there who want to answer your questions and offer their advice. So reach out! Write them an email or give them a call. Some of these adults may be at your school or in your community. Or you may need to look further. Search for cyberbullying experts online. If you read a great article in a newspaper or magazine, contact the writer. Talk about the issues and invite him or her to offer advice. The expertise and guidance of these adults can help you make a difference at your school.

Get the Scoop at Your School

Once you've learned more about cyberbullying in general, the next step is to figure out what's going on at your school specifically. Do you know how much cyberbullying happens among your fellow students? How does it affect them, and what are they trying to do about it? Do you know if other students feel like the school is doing enough to help end and prevent cyberbullying?

When we talk to teens, we ask them to estimate how many of their classmates have cyberbullied others. We often get answers that range from 70 to 90 percent, or even higher. The perception is that *most* teens cyberbully—yet actually the opposite is true. As we said back in **Chapter 1**, our research has found that fewer than one in five students have ever cyberbullied others, and even fewer (8 percent) had done it in the previous 30 days. Do you know how these numbers compare to what's happening at *your* school? If not, find out! Work together with other teens to administer a survey to students—and then do it again periodically (say, at the beginning or end of each quarter or semester). That way you can keep track of trends and see if the problem is increasing or decreasing. You could do these surveys as a school project, as part of an anti-bullying club, or just because you want to do something meaningful. Consider asking questions like these:

- On what social media sites have you experienced cyberbullying, if any? *(Give a list of options and ask survey-takers to check all that apply.)*

- How did being cyberbullied make you feel? *(Give a list of options and ask survey-takers to check all that apply, from sad and angry to frustrated and embarrassed.)*
- If you've been cyberbullied, who did you tell? *(Again, ask survey-takers to check all that apply on a list.)*

To survey your fellow students, it's a good idea to use Survey Monkey (**surveymonkey.com**) or one of the many other free online tools that allow people to remain anonymous. This will encourage them to be really honest in their answers. Then you can use what you learn to help you and others decide how to respond to cyberbullying at your school. Maybe a lot of people are dealing with problems on a specific social media site. Perhaps others are fed up with all the online drama among certain students. Maybe still others are hesitant to tell adults about cyberbullying situations affecting them or others. Whatever you learn, share your findings with your fellow students through an anonymous blog, a Twitter account, or other online site. Also tell teachers, counselors, and school administrators what you've learned. Having facts and figures to back up your suggestions and ideas for solutions will help you show how important it is to do whatever it takes to make things better.

Think About It

Q: Search online for news reports of three recent cyberbullying incidents in your state or province. Why do you think these specific situations happened? Was the cyberbullying in these cases similar to what you see at your school?

Review the Rules

When you have a good idea of the cyberbullying problems your school is facing, take some time to figure out how the school typically responds in these situations. Because of laws passed in the last decade, your school should have a policy about harassment and bullying—most likely including cyberbullying, but not necessarily. Many schools had bullying policies before these laws were around, so if the one at your school is old, it may not mention *cyber*bullying specifically. In addition, the policy might have been written by adults who weren't up to date about what you and other students deal with online, so it may leave out some important points. Start by looking at your student handbook. If you don't see anything there that specifically talks about bullying or cyberbullying, ask a counselor or your principal if you can see your school's bullying policy. If you feel that it's not easy enough to find the policy, you might suggest that your school post a copy online so that other students can be more aware of what it says and what it covers.

If your school's policy has some of these flaws or deficiencies, you can help make it better. Start by finding out exactly what the policy *does* say. Read it carefully and focus on the information about cyberbullying and the misuse of technology. Do you feel that it's adequate? Think about specific incidents you've experienced or witnessed involving students (from your school or others), and consider whether the policy would address those situations. Does it cover the types of social media, devices, and other technologies that you and other students are using? Do you have suggestions about what could or should be added or changed?

Also, the policy might address how school officials should respond to bullying incidents, as well as what they are doing to prevent such incidents in the first place. Would you say that what they're doing is working well? Not so well? Not at all? Why? What kinds of improvements would make the policy more effective?

Once you've read the policy and thought about what it says, share your feedback with the school. Be honest, but also be constructive with your criticism. You and a few other students could meet with an administrator to discuss how the policy can and should be updated. Respectfully point out problems and missing pieces that you see, and offer specific ideas and alternative solutions. Alone or with the help of fellow students, you could also write a brief, informative memo to the school administration explaining your suggestions and the reasons behind them. For example, you might point out that the types of consequences the current policy calls for don't prevent many kids from being cruel online, but that you have ideas for other strategies you think would work better. Also ask the administration to follow up with you after they've read your memo. You want to be sure that your ideas and thoughts are being heard and considered. If you're concerned about this, one option would be to get a parent to sign off on the

> BE SURE THAT YOUR IDEAS AND THOUGHTS ARE BEING HEARD AND CONSIDERED.

memo, which might motivate the administration to respond to you promptly. You could also run your ideas by a favorite teacher or other adult at school to see if they would be willing to support your recommendations. A school adult could, for example, help you set up a meeting with the appropriate person to speak with. Your suggestions could end up making your school a better place!

Take Action!

Once you've learned more about cyberbullying and about what's going on at your school, it's time to take that knowledge to the next level. This section gives you suggestions for activities to increase respect at your school and to show that bullying—in any form—is not welcome. Some of these could be one-time events, while others are ongoing projects. And don't stop here. Brainstorm. Talk to friends. Search online to find out what other people have done. The possibilities are endless!

Join the Club

Many students in middle school or high school have been part of at least one school organization or club. Some clubs focus on athletics, others emphasize academics, and still others get members involved in community service, social issues, or other activities. And a new and growing kind of club is dedicated to ending bullying and creating a positive, respectful atmosphere at school.

If your school already has an anti-bullying club, join in. If not, start one. Club activities can include coming up with ideas to increase respect among all students, to condemn hate and cruelty, and to make kindness go viral. Some anti-bullying clubs hold events to teach students more about cyberbullying and online safety, and to share stories about bullying (online and off) and its aftermath. Adults often try to do these things, too, but as a student *you* have the most power and potential to really change things. *You* know and understand the issues, pressures, worries, and dilemmas that you and other teens face. By joining or founding an anti-bullying club, you can tackle these challenges and improve your school, one person at a time.

It Takes One

These stories from students describe the activities of an anti-bullying club at Cumberland Valley High School in Mechanicsburg, Pennsylvania. The club is called the "It Takes One" (ITO) club. Maybe their experiences will give you ideas for your own club.

ITO focuses on the prevention and awareness of bullying and all other forms of harassment. We emphasize the fact that it only takes one active bystander to defuse and prevent these types of conflicts. During club meetings, we frequently host guest speakers. We also do team-building activities and games. We hope these meetings will not only help give students the courage to stand up for one another, but also help them understand each other's point of view.

—Eden Klepper, 17

As a club started to prevent bullying, ITO has grown to represent so much more. A safe haven for students who feel left out during the school day, a place to laugh with friends after class, somewhere to relax before the stress of homework begins, and an all-around judgment-free zone are all ideals ITO represents. Students feel safe coming to our club meetings because they know they can be themselves, which unfortunately seems to be a change for many high school students. Whether we're watching movies, bowling, making ice-cream sundaes, or studying the effects of being a positive bystander, the leaders and members of the ITO club strive to foster a school culture in which students feel comfortable being themselves and standing up for others.

—Taylor Barber, 17

ITO has broadened our school's views on bullying. We've helped our peers understand that bullying is no longer an act that can be defined by a single action. Through the club's meetings and announcements, we've also taught each other that the school is a family. We look after each other, and we stand up for one another as if we were brothers or sisters. ITO has educated students, staff, and advisors on the importance of identifying an act of bullying and on how anyone can be the "one"—the one who takes the first step in preventing bullying.

—Nathan Tran, 17

First and foremost, the ITO club instills in its members and the entire school the positive message of respecting all people. Yes, we advocate people becoming active bystanders so that bullying behavior can be thwarted, but we have a deeper goal: to show students the power of being respectful. I have seen this come to fruition through the class meetings at school and our club meetings. The presence of our club pushes people to see the consequences of their actions. That will not only help people end bullying, but it will also make people better citizens.

—Mike Casciotti, 17

Be a Mentor

Growing up I would always talk to my older brother about problems that I didn't feel comfortable talking to my mom about. Most kids feel more comfortable talking to another teen, because they feel that person has been through the same thing.

—Kai, 18, Florida

Everybody has the power to help delete cyberbullying and encourage others to be kinder. As a matter of fact, you probably already influence the behavior of your friends, fellow students, and other people in many small ways every day, and they probably influence you, though you may not always realize it. If you'd like to take this influence a step further, look into becoming a peer mentor. Peer mentors are students who advise and guide others as they deal with difficult problems and stressful situations, including cyberbullying. Find out whether your school already has a peer mentoring program. If it doesn't, talk to a teacher, counselor, or administrator about starting one. Explain that peer mentoring can be a great way not only to build a kinder and more respectful school in general, but also to spread important information and messages about cyberbullying and other kinds of bullying. And let them know that research has proven that if peer mentoring is done well, it really makes a positive difference.

In addition, bullying tends to have a more negative effect on people who are isolated than on those who have strong support from friends and others around them. Peer mentoring can help build that support and create an environment where students know they have each other's backs. As this idea grows, people who see cyberbullying happen are less likely to consider it someone else's problem. They'll realize that cyberbullying affects *everyone*, regardless of who's being targeted. In turn, they'll take steps to fight bullying in all its forms.

As a mentor, you might:

- Remind the person you're mentoring that he or she isn't alone in experiencing cyberbullying, or in feeling the pain and loneliness it can cause.
- Encourage him or her to speak up and not be silent when experiencing or witnessing cyberbullying.
- Share a story about cyberbullying that the person may be able to relate to. This could be something you've experienced or seen yourself, or something you've heard or read about in the news.
- Talk about positive ways to resolve conflicts.
- Discuss ways to stay safe online, and talk honestly about how this can be harder than it sounds.
- Most important, just be available to listen, talk, and provide support and encouragement.

Mentoring can be a one-on-one activity, but it also works well in small groups. For example, you could hold a mentoring group at a specific table in the cafeteria during lunch, or in a classroom during after-school hours. With a small group, you can get a little extra creative in the ways you talk about cyberbullying and other topics. Perhaps to start a conversation about different ways to address harassment and hate, you could act out scenarios and have people take turns playing various roles.

In addition, part of peer mentoring can involve offering support and advice to younger students in your community. Because you know the potential problems kids could run into online as they grow older, and because they probably look up to you, you're in a great

Case by Case

A great way to start a conversation in a mentoring meeting (or anywhere, for that matter!) is to read and consider case studies—real examples of cyberbullying. This gets people thinking practically about cyberbullying. It encourages them to consider exactly how they'd respond if they were the person being targeted, how they'd help if it happened to someone they cared about, and how such a situation might be avoided or prevented in the future. Talking this out one-on-one or in a small group gives people a chance to voice their thoughts and discuss constructive ways to handle problems. That way, if something similar happens in real life to you, one of your friends, or a fellow student, you'll already have thought about ways to respond.

position to help them avoid these situations before they happen. Start by asking teachers or principals from your former middle or elementary school if you could visit and talk to current students about using technology safely and responsibly. Share with those students some of what you've learned from your own experiences online or the experiences of friends. Talk with them about why it's important to avoid putting too much private information online, and remind them to be careful about who they interact with in cyberspace. Emphasize that you never *really* know who you're communicating with unless you can see him or her in real time. Also encourage them to confide in adults they trust if they have problems, questions, or worries.

Another important way to mentor others is through your actions. Always show integrity online and off, and try to use good judgment in all that you say and do. Others in your life—especially those younger than you—are paying attention to how you act to get a feel for what *is* and *isn't* okay for teens to do. No one's perfect, of course. But if you do your best, people will notice.

> *I've started to talk to other kids who have had similar experiences. I try and help them because they're going through the same thing that I went through, and it helps to talk to people who understand.*
>
> —Steven, 13, United Kingdom

Walk the Walk

Community walks, runs, or bike rides are often held to increase awareness of an issue and to raise money for a cause, such as finding a cure for cancer, saving the rainforests, or supporting kids with autism. You can hold a similar event built on a "Spread Kindness" or "Stand Up to Bullying" platform. It could be a 5K run, a stroll through town, or a walk around the school track.

Advertise your event with flyers, signs, online posts, banners, and anything else you can think of to spread the word and share your message. Try to get local businesses to sponsor the event. For instance, shops might pay to print T-shirts in exchange for having their logos or slogans on them. Invite the local press, including people who work for the newspaper, the local TV news, and the local radio station. Do whatever it takes to get a lot of people to participate and pay attention. Make your event turn heads, and get people talking and asking

Think About It

Q: What is one thing you could do this week to make cyberbullying less of a problem at your school?

Q: Do you think it's possible to *completely* end cyberbullying at your school? Why or why not?

questions about why you're doing what you're doing. They may be inspired to help raise awareness and make a difference themselves!

Make an Announcement

If you have a strong anti-cyberbullying message, one great way to get it out there is by making a public service announcement (PSA). PSAs are typically short, creative, informative videos designed to bring attention to a problem. Many also encourage viewers to work toward resolving that problem, and may offer suggestions for doing so. You've probably seen at least one online. Maybe you've even thought to yourself that you could do something similar. Well, you can—and it isn't as hard as you might think.

For one thing, you don't need fancy equipment to make a great PSA. If your school has a digital video camera that you can borrow and use, that's great. But even if it doesn't, you can use your phone or tablet, or borrow one from a friend or relative. Plus, PSAs are fun to make! Recruit your friends and acquaintances to help, and make the most of their skills, talents, and interests. Brainstorm a slogan, plot, or general outline of what you want your PSA to cover. Perhaps someone with a flair for language can compose the script. A friend who's great with software could edit the video after you shoot it. Someone who loves to draw can help create any art you might want to include. And your friends who love acting and public speaking can take the starring roles on-screen. As you plan and rehearse, be sure to also think about backdrops and where you'll shoot different scenes. Keep in mind that a standard PSA can be as short as 30 seconds. Yours can be as long as a few minutes, depending on what you want to cover, but make sure not to drag it out too long. Just focus on making it as engaging and hard-hitting as possible.

Once you've made your video, upload it to YouTube, TeacherTube, SchoolTube, or a similar site. Use social media to share the video link with everyone you know. Look into showing your PSA in a class, at a school assembly, or through the school's daily video announcements. Look beyond your school, too. Many companies and organizations sponsor PSA contests specifically for middle and high school students. Look around for these contests and find out how to submit your creation.

If video just isn't your thing, your PSA can take another form. It might be a poster that includes art, photos, quotes from people who have been bullied or have bullied others, or other relevant information. Or maybe you'd rather write and record a short, catchy song that tells a story about cyberbullying. The important thing is to share the information with others in a powerful way that will get them to stop, think, and care about cyberbullying.

> GET PEOPLE TO STOP, THINK, AND CARE ABOUT CYBERBULLYING.

Host a Poetry Slam

Writing can be a great way to express feelings, explore ideas, and work through difficult situations and personal problems. And whether it takes the form of diary entries, journals, blogs, essays, short stories, poems, or other writing, it can also be a way of coping with the injustice and pain you see in the world around you.

Some writing will always stay private. But many people also like to share some of their work with others. One way to do this is at poetry slams or other open-mike events where people read their work aloud in a supportive, welcoming, and respectful setting. You could create that setting and *also* start an important conversation by organizing a reading focused on the topics of respect, kindness, bullying, and cyberbullying. Look into holding the event in your school's auditorium, at a local coffeehouse, or at a public library, youth-group setting, or community center. Try to get a few friends to sign up right away so you know you'll have some people to start off the evening. Search YouTube for "poetry slam" or "open-mike reading" to get a feel for how these events work. And then spread the word! Hang up flyers across campus. Post information and reminders online. Tell friends to tell their friends. Encourage people to just come and listen, or to participate as readers.

> WORDS ARE NOT *JUST* WORDS. THEY CAN WOUND. THEY CAN ALSO HEAL.

Sharing thoughts, experiences, and feelings through writing can be a really effective way to show that words are not *just* words. They can wound—causing anger, hurt, betrayal, sadness, or rejection. They can also heal, by conveying encouragement, support, kindness, comfort, and hope. Use an event like this to open other people's eyes to the pain that cyberbullying causes and to the support students can offer one another.

Take Center Stage

Digital drama is a pain. But other kinds of drama can be entertaining, thought-provoking, and even inspiring. So if you have a flair for the theatrical, use your skills to get people thinking and talking about cyberbullying and its effects. Produce a skit or play and perform it for a class, in the auditorium, or at an after-school club. If you need help getting actors, props, and other elements together, turn to your school's theater department (if it has one). Or maybe you have creative friends who are excited about the idea of staging a short performance. With their help or on your own, write a bullying or cyberbullying storyline that is interesting, clear, and powerful. It could even be based on a real incident that happened in your community, or one that got a lot of media attention somewhere else.

It takes guts to put yourself out there like this. But it can have a big payoff. Some people in the audience will know you or other actors, or will at least have seen you in class or passed you in the hallways. This personal connection can bring home your message and make it even more effective. Seeing someone they know being hurt (even if it's only an act), as opposed to a stranger on the news, will help viewers put themselves in the shoes of people who are being bullied and show them that it can

> **IT TAKES GUTS TO PUT YOURSELF OUT THERE. BUT IT CAN HAVE A BIG PAYOFF.**

happen here, at their school. In turn, they'll better understand how cyberbullying can wreck lives—for everybody involved—and how students themselves can help turn this around. Your production can leave a long-lasting impression, and it can help change how everyone treats each other, both at school and online.

Move Beyond Your School

When it comes to deleting cyberbullying, think *big*. You don't need to restrict your efforts to your school alone. You can reach a broader audience by working with school district administrators to organize anti-cyberbullying efforts at other schools, or by writing a letter to major newspapers in your area. You can contact your state, provincial, or national legislators to find out what they're doing to address cyberbullying, and to encourage them to make the topic a priority. These and many other ventures will help you increase the number of people—of all ages—who will benefit from what you're doing.

Speak Up

The lessons you've learned and applied at your school could also help make life better for students at other schools in your area. So take what you've found out and share it with people at the other schools in your district, city, or town. You could:

- Coordinate events and activities with students at other schools. By combining resources, you can have an even bigger impact in your community.

- Interact with upper-level administrators such as curriculum directors or technology specialists. Fill them in on the specific circumstances at your school, and suggest ways to apply that knowledge to programs at other schools.

- Attend and participate in school board meetings and other area or district-level meetings, especially if the topic of bullying, cyberbullying, or online safety is on the agenda.

Remember, if you don't speak up, you can't be sure that the adults in charge *really* know what's going on. Hearing your perspective will help them understand more about how their decisions affect you and other students. Tell them about what you've done at your school to reduce cyberbullying so that they'll see examples of how problems can be managed well. Remind them that the benefits of technology outweigh the risks. And let them know what still needs to be done.

Throughout high school, I've been a student representative on the Educational Technology Advisory Committee (ETAC). The committee's purpose is to recognize priorities for school technology programs, and also identify ways technology can enhance learning. One goal we've focused on is emphasizing cyber safety practices among staff and students, and defining a strategy to raise awareness of these practices.

To meet this goal, we formed a Cyber Safety Committee. The committee has led a workshop for secondary schools, and another workshop for parents. The secondary schools' workshop brought together groups of staff and students from each middle and high school to learn more about cyber safety and cyberbullying. Each school's group identified issues their school was facing. Then they went back to their schools and shared what they'd learned with the rest of the staff and the students.

The second major project was putting on a parents' night, open to any parent in the district. This gave parents the opportunity to hear from a panel of students who answered questions about cyberbullying, text messaging, Internet safety, social networking, and interactive video gaming. Parents could also attend a breakout session put on by local law enforcement discussing the legal consequences of sexting, making threats online or by text, and other misuses of technology. There was so much interest in the first parents' night that we had to limit the number of attendees because of space!

I've co-led several of these workshops. Having a leadership position in my school district has given me a way to voice the needs of students, and to help make positive change. I've found that when you have a dedicated team of faculty, they're really willing to listen to what you have to say, and ready to take action on it.

—Kylie LeMay, 18, Colorado

Write a Letter to the Editor

A good way to bring the issue of cyberbullying to more people in your community is to write a letter to the editor of your local newspaper. Newspapers don't have room to print all the letters they get, but if you take the time to compose a well-written, thoughtful essay about cyberbullying, it will probably have a good chance of getting published. For one thing, the topic of bullying affects and interests a lot of people. In addition, your letter will stand out if you include real-life, direct experiences. While you should not name names, you *can* describe an actual cyberbullying situation from your school, which will make it clear to readers that cyberbullying is going on right around them—perhaps to people they know and care about. In addition to explaining how cyberbullying affects you and others, be sure to write about what needs to be done to fight cyberbullying. Encourage others in the community to offer their help and support. Your letter might inspire someone who hasn't thought much about this issue to step up and get involved.

Write from the Heart
If you like, you could ask a parent, writing teacher, or other person to read your letter to check for typos, make suggestions, or give other feedback before you send it in. But make sure the words and ideas are truly yours. A letter that comes from your heart will be more interesting than one that repeats someone else's thoughts.

Get Political

The 49 U.S. states with anti-bullying laws (all but Montana) require schools to have policies prohibiting bullying. Most of these policies refer specifically to cyberbullying, although only a few explicitly acknowledge that schools can respond to online harassment that happens away from campus. In Canada, some provinces and territories have similar laws.

Many states and provinces also have other laws that can come into play in certain cyberbullying situations. Extreme incidents— whether they involve teens or adults—can fall under existing criminal laws about harassment or stalking. In other cases, a person might sue someone for intentionally inflicting emotional harm, or for spreading damaging lies. Do you know exactly what *your* state's laws say about cyberbullying? If not, find out. Go to your state government's website. Visit the library and research the law there. Talk with a government or history teacher at your school. You can also check out **wordswound.org/laws** for the latest news about cyberbullying laws.

Think hard about what you're learning. Do you believe the law is appropriate, adequate, and effective? If you have any concerns, let your local, state, and national legislators know. For example, does the law include language specifically discussing online bullying? Does it make it clear that educators can, in some cases, take action against cyberbullying even if it didn't happen at school? Does it *require* schools to do certain things, or does it just make vague suggestions? If your state law doesn't contain these important elements, educate your lawmakers and representatives about these missing pieces. Let them know how the laws can do a better job of safeguarding you and other students.

"We Feel Trapped"

This letter from Amelia, a Wisconsin high school student, describes her experiences with cyberbullying. Amelia didn't sit by after being bullied. She wanted to help others who had been in her situation. So she spoke up and wrote to her state legislator to ask for change.

My name is Amelia. I'm a junior in high school. I am writing this because I'm concerned that Wisconsin has no laws dealing directly with cyberbullying. According to statistics from the Cyberbullying Research Center, 10 to 20 percent of teens in America experience cyberbullying regularly. I am one of those 10 to 20 percent. Speaking for myself and other bullied teens, we feel trapped.

In my experience with cyberbullying, I've learned that it never stops. Nothing has ever made me feel as vulnerable and rejected as my experiences with cyberbullying. Eighth grade was the worst for me. My three best friends hacked into my MySpace profile and deleted everything. They replaced my info with statuses about my sexuality and the way I looked. They also deleted all my photos and replaced them with pictures of porn stars. I deleted my profile to try and get away from all of it. But the next day one of the girls punched me in the face while the others watched. I told the principal everything, but the only thing the girls were punished for was hitting me. Those girls made me afraid to be at school, and there seemed to be nothing my school could do about it. That fact made me feel helpless and trapped. Then high school started. Something mean and hurtful was posted about me online at least monthly all the way through my freshman and sophomore years. It was always by the same group of people. I blocked them from my account so I couldn't see what they were saying. But that still didn't stop them.

The summer before my junior year, I was being bullied and threatened so badly I had to change my phone number. When my junior year started, I felt like everyone's target. No matter what I do, there's a post about me at least weekly. It was all on Facebook, so I blocked all the people I don't trust and created a Twitter account. But it followed me there, too. I've asked the school for help, but they say they can't do anything about it because it happens online. I am afraid of these people. I am threatened by them and then I have to go to school and sit in classes with them. Since the school couldn't do anything, I went to the police. But when I asked for their help they didn't know what to do either.

I try to ignore these things. I am a strong and confident person. But this year I've hit my breaking point. I can't keep going through this. I can't be afraid to go to school, and I shouldn't have to be afraid to be myself. I feel like an outcast at my school and it's all because of cyberbullying. I don't know what else I can do, so now I am coming to you for your help.

The only law Wisconsin has for dealing with cyber harassment is the "unlawful use of computerized communication systems" (947.0125). Many other states first enacted laws against cyberbullying due to suicides caused in part by cyberbullying. I feel like we shouldn't let our state get to this point. We should not wait for someone to be hurt so badly that they feel like they need to end their life. It's time to be proactive with this issue. Something needs to be done.

Amelia's letter resulted in her legislator proposing changes to state law. One voice *can* make a difference, so be sure that yours is heard.

Take the First Step

As you can see, there are many different ways you can help make your school and community a cyberbully-free place. Some require a fair amount of time and energy on your part, but a number of them do not. Some of them can be done on your own, while others are best organized with a group of your friends and maybe the help of an adult who cares about this issue. Size up your specific situation, figure out what actions you think will fit best, and then give one of the ideas in this chapter a shot! Don't be afraid to get creative and play around with these examples and suggestions so they work for you and your situation, school, or community. Use your imagination, and be bold. When a great idea comes to you, take it and run with it as far as it will go!

"Reach out to those people who are sitting at the cafeteria by themselves, or if they don't have many friends . . . you should sit with them, you should talk to them, get to know them, because they're just like you. Everybody has insecurities, everybody has fears."
—Joe Jonas

??? Status Update: Have or Have Not

As you've read, there are many ways to show kindness to others in small ways—and many ways others can show kindness to us. Read the following list and mark whether you or your friends have or have not done each nice thing for someone else, or if someone else has or has not done them for you sometime in the last month. How many "haves" are you seeing? If you don't think it's enough, consider what more you could be doing and what you can encourage friends to do.

1. I've praised someone for something he or she accomplished.	☐ I HAVE ☐ HAVE NOT
2. I've told someone how handsome or pretty he or she is.	☐ I HAVE ☐ HAVE NOT
3. I've said "thank you" to someone.	☐ I HAVE ☐ HAVE NOT
4. I've offered my help to someone.	☐ I HAVE ☐ HAVE NOT
5. I've made someone laugh out loud (LOL).	☐ I HAVE ☐ HAVE NOT
6. I've stood up for a friend who was being mistreated online.	☐ I HAVE ☐ HAVE NOT
7. I've reported something inappropriate online to an adult.	☐ I HAVE ☐ HAVE NOT
8. I've apologized to someone online when I was in the wrong.	☐ I HAVE ☐ HAVE NOT
9. I've acted as a mediator to help my friends solve a conflict.	☐ I HAVE ☐ HAVE NOT

10. I've spoken my mind despite what others may think of me.	☐ I HAVE ☐ HAVE NOT
11. I've worked with friends to support others and to discourage people from cyberbullying.	☐ I HAVE ☐ HAVE NOT
12. I've been part of a club or other activity that fights cyberbullying.	☐ I HAVE ☐ HAVE NOT

What is one of the nicest things you have done for someone else online?

_____

_____

_____

_____

_____

_____

1. Someone has praised me for an accomplishment I've achieved.	☐ THEY HAVE ☐ HAVE NOT
2. Someone has told me how pretty or handsome I am.	☐ THEY HAVE ☐ HAVE NOT
3. Someone has said "thank you" to me.	☐ THEY HAVE ☐ HAVE NOT
4. Someone has offered to help me with something.	☐ THEY HAVE ☐ HAVE NOT
5. Someone has made me laugh or smile.	☐ THEY HAVE ☐ HAVE NOT

6. Someone has stood up for me when I was being mistreated online. ☐ THEY HAVE ☐ HAVE NOT

7. Someone has apologized to me when he or she was in the wrong. ☐ THEY HAVE ☐ HAVE NOT

8. Someone has acted as a mediator to help me resolve a conflict. ☐ THEY HAVE ☐ HAVE NOT

9. Someone has taken the time to ask if I was okay and show that he or she cares. ☐ THEY HAVE ☐ HAVE NOT

10. Someone has made me feel good. ☐ THEY HAVE ☐ HAVE NOT

11. People at my school or in my community have worked to fight bullying. ☐ THEY HAVE ☐ HAVE NOT

12. A school club or other group has tried to make my school a kinder place. ☐ THEY HAVE ☐ HAVE NOT

What is one of the nicest things that someone else has done for you online?

_____

_____

_____

_____

_____

_____

_____

Chapter 7

Make Kindness Go Viral

The number of suicidal, depressed friends I have is ridiculous. I'm not saying anything against them—they are amazing, caring, loving people. No, I'm saying something against the people who think it's okay to put my friends in that state. I'm not the nicest person either, but never once have I told someone to "go kill themselves" or that I "truly hate them." Cyberbullying is the worst because people feel comfortable sitting at a keyboard, instead of saying something face-to-face. It's all over the place. If I see someone being picked on or laughed about at school I will private message them on Facebook saying that they can talk to me anytime. I always say that if they're down they can come and stay with me. My door is always open. I've become a rock for a lot of people.

—Jordan, 15, New Zealand

One of the things that makes cyberbullying so especially painful is the fact—or the feeling, at least—that *everyone* is in on the joke. If someone posts an embarrassing picture of you on Instagram or a hurtful comment about you on Facebook, you feel like everybody sees it. On top of that, a post can spread so widely and so quickly that it can seem like there's almost no way to stop it. Stories about bullying have always

"The most important thing we can all do is to treat each other with kindness and respect. If you see a kid being picked on, you make sure you stand up for him."
—*President Barack Obama, speaking to 10-year-old "Kid President" Robby Novak*

spread rapidly through school hallways, of course. But technology has definitely made this happen even faster, and spread more widely. So why not turn things around—why not use the power of technology to do some good? Take advantage of all of the tech tools at your disposal to make kindness go viral. Show others that it's cool to care. In this chapter, you'll read about lots of examples that we've seen or learned about from students at schools across North America and beyond. Think about how these ideas might work at your school or in your community, and then get started!

> *I learned that two people can come up with an idea, run with it, and it can do wonders.*
>
> —Travis, 17, Nova Scotia, Canada

Promote Kindness at Your School and Beyond

Kindness matters. You probably appreciate it when others are kind to you—when you're already having a good day, and *especially* if you're having a bad day. You've probably paid kindness forward by being nice, respectful, or helpful to others. And we've all heard about random acts of kindness—doing something nice for a complete stranger for no other reason than to brighten someone's day. Other times kindness isn't so random. Research shows that people who see an act of kindness or compassion are much more likely to be kind and compassionate immediately afterward. Also, kindness seems to have a bigger impact when it's specific and focused, instead

> "When I was in 7th grade, I remember being picked on all the time. If you can, realize that the things that people say about you don't really matter. It gets better. People get nicer, too."
> —Stephen Colbert

of general. For example, people are more likely to give to antipoverty organizations whose commercials show specific children in need rather than those whose commercials share the big and general idea that millions and millions of people are hungry and struggling.

So what does all this have to do with you and your school? Sometimes, when you confront a huge challenge, it's easy to feel like there's no point even trying to make a difference unless you can change the world in some legendary way. But every great movement started with one small action. Standing up for one person who is bullied is that kind of action. Showing compassion toward somebody who's having a hard time is another one. Don't be afraid to think big, but be okay with (and even excited about) starting small! Soon you may find that the best thing about these kinds of actions is that they grow when other people see them. You don't have to make a big, public deal out of what you're doing. Just be kind, and know that you're making a positive difference in someone else's life. Others will find out about it, and others will see it—if not the first time, then maybe the second, or third. Eventually, your actions will start a domino effect leading to someone else doing the same thing—being kind. You'll see that kindness can be contagious. It just takes one person, and then another, and then another to start a movement that can go viral and change the whole culture and atmosphere of your school.

> **KINDNESS MATTERS.**

Think About It

Q: What is the nicest thing someone has ever done for you? Could you do something like that for someone you know? How about a complete stranger?

Q: Do you think that sometimes people are embarrassed or afraid to be nice? If so, why do you think that is? How could it be changed?

Reach Out

Just reaching out to someone can be one of the most powerful ways to promote kindness. A great example of this comes from Queen Creek High School in Arizona. Chy Johnson, one of the school's sophomores, was being bullied. Because Chy had been born with a brain disorder, she had the cognitive abilities of a third grader. That year at school, other kids were calling her stupid, shoving her, and throwing garbage at her.

Carson Jones, the school's senior quarterback, saw what was going on and didn't think it was right. So he stepped up. With the help of his football teammates Tucker Workman, Colton Moore, and a few others, he set out to support Chy and stop the cruelty. When the players saw Chy sitting alone at lunch, they invited her to sit with them. They walked her to class, and made her an unofficial member of the football team. They made sure to let her know that they had her back.

"I just thought if the other kids saw us treating her nicely, then maybe they'd do the same thing," said Carson. Carson and his teammates proved that kindness—online or off—can catch on. The bullying stopped. (Oh, and by the way—the Queen Creek football team went undefeated in 2012!)

You don't have to wait until someone's being bullied to show him or her kindness. If you see someone who seems lonely, sad, or in need of a boost, try sharing a friendly word with him or her. Ask the person to join you at a club or other activity. Reach out!

Make Art with a Message

Are you the artistic type? Maybe you're skilled in drawing or painting. Maybe you love to take photos and make collages. Put your talents to work and design posters to encourage others to be kind and to end cyberbullying. Combine your art with catchy slogans and vivid colors. Let your imagination run wild! The more creative your poster is, the more it will stand out. After all, your classrooms and hallways are probably full of posters inviting people to care about issues, support causes, or take part in events. So work to give your poster a unique angle. It might encourage others to be upstanders instead of bystanders when they see bullying. It could ask other people to focus on kindness, not cruelty. Or it might emphasize school pride and remind people that bullying and cyberbullying aren't what your school is all about.

You could also personalize your posters with information specific to your school. For example, you might use data you gathered from a survey: "70% of Silverhawks step up and report those who harass others on social media!" or "85% of East students think our school could use more kindness." Or maybe you'll interview students or staff and include their quotes, advice, or anecdotes about kindness versus cruelty. Whatever your focus is, a well-made poster with a clear and powerful message can get students to stop, think, and reflect on their own ideas and actions.

Take the Pledge

Another way to encourage kindness and fight cyberbullying at your school is to start a pledge campaign. Begin by thinking of a creative slogan or catchphrase. Work to make it memorable and fairly short, like "Niceness Is Priceless," "Think Before You Type," or "If You Wouldn't Say It In Person, Don't Say It Online." Brainstorm with friends, classmates, or members of your school's anti-bullying club to come up with something great.

Once you have your phrase figured out, ask permission to hang a large pledge banner in a hallway or other common area at school.

Title it with your slogan and write something like, "Take the Pledge: I will choose kindness over meanness, online and off!" Students who agree can sign their names. At first, maybe only a few students will sign. But hopefully many others will think about the pledge and soon join in. Depending on the size of your school, you could print every student's name on the poster next to a blank space for the signature. If students see blank spots next to their names because they haven't signed the pledge yet—and if they see that lots of others *have* signed—it may encourage them to get on board.

If you want to take your pledge campaign to the next level, consider raising funds to spread your message further. You could put on a carwash, hold a walk-a-thon, or ask local businesses to sponsor your project. Then you can use the money you earn to make T-shirts, buttons, pins, key chains, magnets, or bumper stickers featuring your message. Finally, make some noise and get even more people to take—and share—the pledge! Invite everyone to wear their shirts on the same day, or to walk around with pins on their backpacks or jackets. Maybe you can gather a group to carry signs with your pledge slogan in a busy place such as the school grounds at the end of the day. Or move beyond the walls of the school and take your pledge to the mall or the city hall! That way parents, other adults, and kids who don't go to your school can learn about your campaign and what you stand for.

I've had to deal with some really horrible bullying and cyberbullying. But I've tried to fight the good fight and to do something about it on a bigger scale, especially because I kept meeting others who were struggling, too. With my mind and heart heavy due to my situation and that of others, I started to research cyberbullying. Ryan Halligan, Megan Meier, Jeffrey Johnston, and more and more names *kept coming up. Reading their stories and the decisions they made to end their cyberbullying cut me deeply. I remembered an organization my mom had told me about called **DoSomething.org**. It's a place for kids and teens to do something to better the world. I decided to create Unbreakable, a project to help me heal as well as heal others who were bullied. I didn't have much of a plan at first—I just knew my goal was to end cyberbullying.*

Soon, I got more passionate and wanted to tell more people what was happening. I wanted to be a voice for all victims of bullying. I printed out hundreds of pages of websites made just to attack kids. I sent a letter describing myself, my Unbreakable project, stories of suicide, and pages and pages of bullying sites to media outlets, politicians, law enforcement, celebrities, school superintendents, and anyone else I hoped would listen. The **Tampa Tribune,** **ABC News,** *and* **Bay News 9** *responded. Soon I was on a media train with Unbreakable. I created an Unbreakable Facebook fan page. My page targeted cyberbullies and the creators of the cruel sites. It also told the stories of Ryan, Megan, and Jeffrey. In the beginning, the page was mostly a surge of congratulations to "whoever this is" speaking out. (Before the media buzz, I didn't tell people that I was behind Unbreakable.) One student who had previously cyberbullied people posted, "I don't know who this is but you are an inspiration to me. Thank you for standing up and speaking out." I think it's awesome that my project has encouraged others to change their ways, and that Unbreakable got a lot more students to think and care about this important issue.*

—Sarah Ball, 17, Florida

Form a Flash Mob

Over the past few years, flash mobs have shown up everywhere from shopping malls to weddings to hit TV shows. Maybe you've seen them yourself: On a seemingly normal day, a big group of people suddenly starts dancing in unison. It seems spontaneous, but in fact it's a carefully planned performance.

Flash mobs are cool, creative, and entertaining. They cause people to stop, watch, and tell others about what they've seen. Videos of them often go viral. They can be just for fun. But because they get so much attention, they can also be used to raise awareness about an issue or an idea—like the idea of spreading kindness and deleting cyberbullying.

One well-known example of an anti-bullying flash mob happened in Vancouver, British Columbia. In honor of Anti-Bullying Day, students from David Lloyd George Elementary and Sir Winston Churchill Secondary schools all went to the mall wearing pink T-shirts emblazoned with the word "Acceptance." They covered their shirts with jackets and hoodies. Then, at a set time, they took off their hoodies and broke out in a dance to Bruno Mars's hit song "Just the Way You Are." The flash mob got lots of attention and highlighted the idea of accepting people for themselves and not bullying others.

Try doing something similar with people at your school. You might be surprised by how many others want to join in! Check out YouTube to see tons of flash mob examples, and use them to come up with a creative idea of your own. And make sure you get someone to record your flash mob performance—we'd love to see it!

Be Creative

People start—and spread—some pretty mean trends online using all the sites, apps, and gadgets that are out there. But you can also take those same tools and use them to spread kindness, understanding, and respect. The ideas in this section are just a few of the ways you can make the most of technology.

Use Memes for Good, Not Evil

Pop culture trends come and go quickly. When technology is involved, that happens even faster. The hot new video, meme, or trending topic can be just brief blips on the radar. For example, everyone was dancing Gangnam Style or doing the Harlem Shake a while back. And as you read this, a new craze has probably taken over. However, if you check out YouTube, you'll still find at least a few Harlem Shake videos made by students to share anti-bullying messages. Some of them are pretty amazing—and have thousands and thousands of views! Think about how you could build on a popular idea—whether it's a new dance, a hit song, or a funny mashup video—to draw attention to spreading kindness or fighting bullying.

Memes are another constantly changing online phenomenon. The most popular memes are usually funny pictures captioned with short phrases. Most memes are just made for a laugh. But others support specific movements, causes, or activities. You could create anti-cyberbullying memes and then get them to catch on by sharing them on your Tumblr, Instagram, or Facebook pages. (There are lots of free meme generators online that you can use to apply your captions or commentary to whatever picture you've chosen.) By harnessing a hot or humorous trend, you can creatively spread your message that kindness beats bullying and that no one ever deserves to be harassed, embarrassed, or mistreated.

The "To Be Kind" Movement

Over the past few years, social media has boomed. But as its popularity grows, so does the ability to mistreat others through the Internet. Often, there's a feeling of hopelessness when it comes to bullying. Some people assume that it's a problem that will always exist. We seek to destroy that mentality by showing the power of kindness, both in person and online. We're optimistic that we can eliminate bullying step-by-step. After a terrifying experience when an online hit list threatened our students and faculty, our Leadership class knew they wanted to make a change. After a long class discussion, someone suggested using social media as a way to help solve the bullying problem rather than make it worse. We decided to use the already trending idea of "to be honest," where users on Facebook can like someone's status and then receive an honest statement from him or her. Using the same format, we changed the idea to "to be kind." Users still take part by liking a post on someone's page. Then the original poster is supposed to give a compliment or write words of kindness on the wall of whoever liked the status. To Be Kind, or TBK, is a simple idea: Treat others as you would wish to be treated. Every one of us possesses the ability to be kind. This simplicity is the answer to preventing bullying.

The impact on our school was instantaneous. TBK turned into a buzz overnight. The very next day after we launched our idea, students were talking and trying to figure out what TBK was and where it came from. Using follow-up actions such as putting positive messages in lockers, we quickly turned it into a movement that lots of people wanted to be part of.

Like many new things, our idea hasn't always been met with positivity. Many of the kind posts that students make on social media are rejected. Many people aren't used to kindness anymore. We're used to ridicule rather than compliments. So sometimes people post negativity in response. When that happens, we just thank them for expressing their feelings, or we ignore the comment. The purpose of TBK isn't to instigate fighting or rumors, or to provide an outlet for people to criticize others. Its purpose is to show that social media and other everyday interactions can be improved with a few thoughtful words. Anyone, of any age, can spread a few extra smiles in a day. And TBK isn't focused solely on students. We encourage parents and community members to get involved and to support our project at work and at home. We've also included the school faculty and staff by sharing words of kindness with them.

We take huge pride in TBK. It has grown into a symbol of anti-bullying not only at our school, but in many schools around our district, country, and beyond. For example, our school participates in a German exchange program. We've helped our partner school establish a TBK program, as well. The world wants kindness. People want to be treated as if they matter. That's the ultimate purpose of the program. We know that kindness will continue to spread and bullying will continue to diminish. Remember: Bullying ends where kindness begins, and it begins with you.

—Quinn Solomon, 17
—Joshua Sanchez, 17
—Danielle Soltren, 17

Lake Brantley High School,
Altamonte Springs, Florida

Build an App

If you have programming experience, consider putting your skills to work making an anti-bullying app to promote respect and discourage hate and harassment. For instance, some high school students in Fresno, California, made an app called Bully Blaster. As you play the Bully Blaster game, you fight your way through a barrage of positive and negative words. The goal is to collect the compliments and destroy the insults.

What app ideas do you have? You could build the next big thing and fight bullying at the same time!

Craft a Comic

If you're feeling creative, but flash mobs and memes aren't your thing, you can use the fun and colorful art form of comics to tell your own anti-bullying or pro-kindness story. Websites such as **bitstrips.com**, **marvelkids.marvel.com**, **toondoo.com**, and **pixton.com** give you the tools to create short online comic strips or even full-fledged stories with amazing graphics and features.

When you've created your comic, post it on social media, a blog, or other sites. And don't stop there. The more people talk about the right things to do online, the more people will do those things. So invite other people to make their own comics, too. You could help launch a contest at your school—either as part of a bigger anti-bullying movement, or on your own—and invite students to vote for their favorite comics. The winning creations could be printed in the school newspaper or yearbook, or on the school's website or Facebook page.

Random Acts of Online Kindness

A random act of kindness might mean helping an elderly person cross the street, or giving a couple of bucks to someone in need. Maybe you've read about the couple who paid for another family's lunch at a restaurant. Or the time a Tennessee man pumped and paid for the gas for 80 random people who stopped by one gas station. Maybe you heard about Jonathon Montanez, the high school basketball player who helped a developmentally disabled player from the opposing team score a basket. You might have read the story of Meghan Vogel, a high school distance runner in Ohio who came in last in a race because she helped a competitor who collapsed on the track. Or how about 12-year-old Ian McMillan, who caught a ball at a baseball game and gave it to a younger fan who was upset that he didn't catch it himself? There's no shortage of stories of people doing simple but amazing things to help others.

You can take this idea of random kindness online. That's what people did for Daniel Cui. Daniel was a freshman soccer goalie from Hillsborough, California. During his first season, a lot of students were blaming him and bullying him online for his team losing all of their games. To show support for Daniel, his teammates and dozens of other students changed their Facebook profile pictures to one of him making a great save. Others tagged, liked, and commented on the photo posts to cheer Daniel on. He came back the following year and played with a new sense of confidence, helping his team to many victories.

> "It's strange to have people telling me that this was such a powerful act of kindness . . . I just did what I knew was right."
> —*Meghan Vogel*

Do you know someone who could use this kind of support? Maybe you could give somebody a simple shout-out when you know he or she is having a tough time. You could stand up for a stranger who is being cyberbullied, or you could welcome a new student at school. Whether in person or online, there are many things you can do to express appreciation, show respect, or try to cheer someone up. It will make that person feel better—and you'll probably find that it makes you feel good, too.

Get Social

If you already use social media sites, why not take advantage of the audience on these sites to spread your ideas about kindness? You could create an Instagram account, Tumblr feed, Twitter account, or Facebook page dedicated to sharing your message. You might encourage school spirit, promote respect and tolerance, give props to students who treat others well, share photos and videos of anti-bullying initiatives, and praise responsible online behavior. You could also invite students to post stories about making kindness go viral and to share insights about what makes your school stand out.

A social media presence like this can be a good way to start discussions, exchange ideas, and conduct polls. It can also give parents and other community members a chance to share their thoughts, understand more about what's going on at your school, and get involved in your pro-kindness, anti-bullying efforts. You can write

> USE SOCIAL MEDIA TO SPREAD YOUR IDEAS ABOUT KINDNESS.

posts and share articles showing that most teens are doing the right things online and on their phones. That can help counter the negative ideas that some adults have about how people your age typically act.

Tech Tips

In addition to your social media accounts, you could promote kindness on a blog that you create using WordPress, Blogger, or another free service. If you do start a blog, be sure to promote it using other online accounts. That will help you reach a larger audience with your ideas, especially since most of your friends and classmates are probably already using those sites.

Whatever platforms you use, be sure to set permissions to limit what community members can upload and post. For example, you may want them to be able to respond to your announcements, requests, and photos, but you may *not* want them to be able to upload their own photos and videos. The important thing is to make sure that someone with their own separate agenda doesn't take over the page or profile.

Nice It Forward

More and more people—especially teens—are starting to purposefully use social media to say nice things about others. This push to "Nice It Forward" seems to have started with Kevin Curwick, a high school football player from Osseo, Minnesota. Using the Twitter handle **@OsseoNiceThings**, Curwick started tweeting kind things about his school and classmates. For example, one tweet read, *"Osseo truly wouldn't be the same without him. His energy and outgoing personality make everyone smile."* Another one said, *"The kindest girl I've met without a doubt. What she does for her family and friends is incredible and we love her for it!"*

The idea caught on—not only at Kevin's school but at many others, as well. For example, a student in Wisconsin launched a Twitter account in response to two other accounts that were anonymously tweeting negative information about the school. (Since then, the hurtful accounts have been removed—thanks in part to a student who spoke out against them on Facebook.)

The summer before my senior year, I noticed Twitter pages popping up that associated themselves with high schools and tweeted harsh and offensive things about students at those schools. I was disgusted by the anonymous tweeters' ability to publicly humiliate their classmates for their own entertainment. Eventually, the trend caught on at my school and three pages were created about Osseo Senior High. I wasn't comfortable with this sort of animosity setting the tone for my senior year, and standing by as my classmates were attacked wasn't on my agenda. But it was

#Nice

There are lots of Twitter accounts based on the Nice It Forward idea. A few of them are:

- @ERHSnicewords
- @GNHSNiceThings
- @ComplimentsDC
- @CHHS_Comps
- @ComplimentsCHHS
- @BlakeNiceThings

Does your school have an account like this? We've also seen them on Instagram, Facebook, and other sites. If your school doesn't have one yet, look into starting one. Anonymously commending and complimenting others can really make their day—or week. (And don't forget to connect with us @wordswound!)

difficult to combat this type of bullying for three reasons. First, I didn't know who the tweeters were. Second, it was summer and it would be hard to get the school administration involved. And third, I'm just one person— how could I do anything? Eventually, the answer became simple and clear: The best way to beat a trend of negativity is to create a trend of positivity.

The result was @OsseoNiceThings, a Twitter account striving to do the opposite of the bullying pages: restore confidence in Osseo, bring back a sense of school unity, and show support for all students. Instead of insults, I anonymously posted compliments about classmates ranging from the three-sport athletes to the band kids and everybody in between. I didn't know if the whole school would be on board, but I knew I could make a difference to a few people.

Incredibly enough, the account started to take off with many people retweeting what @OsseoNiceThings had to say. People even messaged me compliments to send out about other students. Eventually, I decided that it was important to share the kindness in other ways, so I created the hashtag #NiceItForward. I based this idea on the "pay it forward" idea of passing on kindness. Nice It Forward encourages all the students getting tweeted about on @OsseoNiceThings to go out and spread kindness in their own ways. I also found that it was really fun to tweet nice things about people and see how it could transform their days. Plus, within a week of the creation of @OsseoNiceThings, the bullying accounts were either deleted or shut down. The atmosphere of Osseo changed, and it was awesome to see a wider variety of students joining in on Osseo Nice. After a couple weeks, a local TV reporter encouraged me to say that I was the account's creator, because he'd seen similar accounts showing up. After the news story broke, many classmates told me that the tweets had made them more comfortable going into the school year.

Running @OsseoNiceThings gave me great opportunities, including appearing on the Steve Harvey Show, *being interviewed by Ryan Seacrest, and having Selena Gomez and Brooklyn Decker tweet their support to me. Even today, the story and the account continue to grow as people from places such as South Korea and Germany send their support. The experience has also allowed me to share the idea of kindness and positivity with others, such as junior high students.*

The most gratifying aspect of @OsseoNiceThings has been proving to myself and to thousands of people around the world how powerful a kind word can be. It has shown me and my school that kindness and positivity are for everyone, and that as soon as we embrace that fact, attitudes can change. Social networking opens up a large audience, and everyone has the opportunity to use that power for hateful comments. Or, as @OsseoNiceThings has shown, social networking can be used to spread positivity around the world.

—Kevin Curwick, 18, Minnesota

Students from West High School in Iowa City, Iowa, are also using social media to promote kindness at their school. Junior Jeremiah Anthony (who you read about on page 5) started the Twitter account **@westhighbros** in 2011 to encourage others at his school. Within a few months, he got some of his friends—his "bros"—to help give others compliments. As of fall 2013, the West High Bros account had over 5,000 followers on Twitter. It also has pages on Facebook and other social media sites.

Another way to Nice It Forward was shown by the Pink Shirt Day movement. It started in 2007 when two Nova Scotia teens wanted to combat hurtful comments being directed toward a freshman who had worn a pink shirt on the first day of school. (One of those teens was Travis, who we quoted at the beginning of this chapter.) Instead of directly confronting the people doing the bullying, two of the school's seniors bought as many pink shirts as they could find and encouraged their classmates to wear pink on the second day of school. The targeted student walked into school that morning to see dozens of his fellow students decked out in pink—a simple but very strong message of support! Since then, the Pink Shirt Day idea has spread across Canada, and beyond, growing to represent an anti-bullying message in general—all because two teens wanted to stand up for a fellow student. Whatever form it takes, Nicing It Forward reminds those who are being bullied that they aren't alone.

Want to Know More?
We've shared lots of ideas and information in this book. There's also a lot more information out there to help you as you work to spread kindness and stop cyberbullying. For a list of up-to-date links and more, visit wordswound.org/resources.

Don't Wait

Kindness is awesome. And being mistreated is awful—whether it happens in a comments thread or in the cafeteria. You get that in your head—after all, it just makes sense. But do you get it in your heart? Maybe you didn't before, but you do now. Whatever your starting point was, we hope that *Words Wound* has inspired you to care more than ever. We've covered everything from the big picture of cyberbullying to how to protect yourself online. We've shown you how to help out as an upstander. Plus, we've given you lots of tools to delete cyberbullying and make kindness go viral.

Now that you have all this information, do something with it! Don't wait. Start creating a positive climate. Work to make your school and community the absolute best they can be. And when the challenges ahead seem overwhelming, remember that every great change starts with just one small step. So take that first step today. And keep in touch. We can't wait to see what you'll do!

Status Update: What Will You Do to Get Started?

You have the ability to change your school for the better, to make it a place where cyberbullying doesn't happen, and to make kindness go viral. So what will you do? On your own or with friends, think about how you'd most like to tackle this challenge. Consider your strengths, skills, talents, and interests. Drop us a note at wordswound.org to tell us what you come up with!

- -

List three specific things you can do to prevent cyberbullying from happening at your school. Choose one idea that you'll commit to doing within the next week.

1. _____

_____

_____

_____

_____

2. _____

_____

_____

_____

_____

3. _____

_____

_____

_____

_____

List three specific ideas for showing kindness to others at your school. Which of the ideas do you think is most likely to make kindness go viral? Which one will you do this week?

1. _____

_____

_____

_____

_____

2. _____

_____

_____

_____

_____

3. _____

_____

_____

_____

_____

Acknowledgments

We are grateful to our families for once again allowing us the time away from our familial duties to research and write this book. Your sacrifice, encouragement, and belief in us continue to propel us forward in pursuing our professional dreams.

We are thankful to our colleagues at our universities for their support and encouragement while working on this book. In addition, the Office of Research and Sponsored Programs at the University of Wisconsin-Eau Claire and the Division of Research at Florida Atlantic University provided valuable resources over the years to help us carry out our work.

We thank the brilliant staff at Free Spirit Publishing, especially Judy Galbraith, Alison Behnke, Tasha Kenyon, and Meg Bratsch, for their perspective, professionalism, and patience.

We also appreciate the amazing relationships we have with caring adults who work tirelessly on behalf of teens. They inspire us to do likewise, and have been staunch supporters of all we do. These individuals include, but are certainly not limited to, Patti Agatston, Emily Bazelon, Anne Collier, Mike Donlin, Dorothy Espelage, David Finkelhor, Molly Gosline, Sue Limber, Larry Magid, Charley Nelson, Sue Scheff, Rachel Simmons, Deborah Temkin, Nancy Willard, and Rosalind Wiseman.

We are most grateful to the hundreds of teens from around the world who shared their stories with us. This book features their voices, experiences, and lives. In particular, we'd like to thank the student leaders who contributed their insights to this work. These include Jeremiah Anthony, Sarah Ball, Kevin Curwick, and Kylie LeMay. We stand boldly and confidently with all of you in your efforts to counter cruelty with kindness, to successfully make it through your adolescence and into a bright future, and to help your peers do the same.

Finally, we would like to thank God for giving us the opportunities and the abilities to make a positive difference in the lives of teens. We feel very blessed to truly and completely love what we do.

—Justin and Sameer

Index

About the Authors

Justin W. Patchin, Ph.D., is a professor of criminal justice in the Department of Political Science at the University of Wisconsin-Eau Claire. He has presented on various topics relating to juvenile justice, school violence, policy and program evaluation, and adolescent Internet use and misuse at academic conferences and training seminars across the United States. He was a futurist in residence in the Behavioral Science Unit of the Federal Bureau of Investigation where he educated officers about the role of law enforcement in preventing and responding to cyberbullying incidents. He has presented at the White House and has appeared on CNN, NPR, and in *Time* and *The New York Times* to discuss issues related to teens' use and misuse of technology. He lives in Wisconsin.

Sameer Hinduja, Ph.D., is a professor in the School of Criminology and Criminal Justice at Florida Atlantic University. He is recognized internationally for his groundbreaking work on the subjects of cyberbullying and safe social networking, concerns that have paralleled the exponential growth in online communication by young people. He works with the U.S. Department of Education and many state departments of education to improve their policies and programming related to the prevention and response of teen technology misuse. He also gives presentations and trainings to teens and youth-serving professionals across the nation to promote the positive and responsible use of the Internet. He lives in Florida.

Justin and **Sameer** are the directors of the Cyberbullying Research Center and the authors of *Bullying Beyond the Schoolyard* and *School Climate 2.0.*

Do you have lots of ideas and opinions? Have you ever seen a book or website and thought, "I'd do that differently"? Then we want to hear from you! We're looking for teens to be part of the Free Spirit Teen Advisory Council. You'll help us keep our books and other products current and relevant by letting us know what you think about things like design, art, and content. Go to www.freespirit.com/teens to learn more and get an application.

Other Great Books from Free Spirit

Vicious
True Stories by Teens About Bullying
edited by Hope Vanderberg of Youth Communication

Essays by teens address bullying: physical, verbal, relational, and cyber. The cruelty and hurt in these stories are unmistakably real—and the reactions of the writers are sometimes cringe-worthy, often admirable, and always believable.
176 pp.; softcover; 5¼" x 7½"

Teen Cyberbullying Investigated
Where Do Your Rights End and Consequences Begin?
by Thomas A. Jacobs, J.D.

Teen Cyberbullying Investigated presents a powerful collection of landmark court cases involving teens and cyberbullying. It asks readers whether they agree with the court's decisions, and urges them to think about how these decisions affect their lives.
208 pp.; softcover; 6" x 9"

Fighting Invisible Tigers
Stress Management for Teens
by Earl Hipp

This book offers proven techniques that teens can use to deal with stressful situations in school, at home, and among friends.
144 pp.; softcover; 2-color; illust.; 6" x 9"

Interested in purchasing multiple quantities and receiving volume discounts? Contact edsales@freespirit.com or call 1.800.735.7323 and ask for Education Sales.

Many Free Spirit authors are available for speaking engagements, workshops, and keynotes. Contact speakers@freespirit.com or call 1.800.735.7323.

For pricing information, to place an order, or to request a free catalog, contact:

Free Spirit Publishing Inc.
217 Fifth Avenue North • Suite 200 • Minneapolis, MN 55401-1299
toll-free 800.735.7323 • local 612.338.2068 • fax 612.337.5050
help4kids@freespirit.com • www.freespirit.com

In eighth grade, I thought I was going to have a great year because I was excited to graduate from grade school. Well, that thought was turned upside down when I got harsh texts from people in my school. Everyone started to hate me and I didn't know why. The next day, my mom went to the school with my phone and showed the principal all the texts I'd gotten from other students. The principal confronted students about it and some of them denied everything while others texted me and apologized. I was so happy I'd gotten some of my friends back. Others were not true friends. I thank my mom so much for telling the principal. I am now a stronger person than I ever imagined I could be. Stand up for yourself. Don't be afraid anymore. You are not alone, and there are others willing to help you.

—Alex, 14, Illinois

I was bullied on Facebook after I moved to a new town. These girls started posting mean things about me and I didn't know what to do. I started cutting myself and became depressed. My grades dropped. When my parents found out what was going on, they talked to my principal for me. They stopped the bullying and got me help.

—Maddie, 16, Texas

I was cyberbullied countless times by someone. Then she got a few more people into it. I thought of many ways to get back at her, but nothing seemed good enough. So then I thought, maybe I'm not good enough. I almost took my life just so none of this would matter anymore. I told my father everything, and he went to the school counselor

When you start feeling this way, it's important to realize that there are people in your life who care—even if you don't always think they do. Start by telling a person you really trust. Think about who you've turned to when you've had problems in the past. If you tell someone and don't feel like she is very helpful or receptive, go to someone else. Don't stop until you find someone who helps you feel better and shows a

GIVE OTHERS A CHANCE TO COME THROUGH FOR YOU.

real determination to help you deal with the bullying. Give others a chance to come through for you. It could make all the difference.

Some teens don't want to tell adults about their experiences with cyberbullying because they think it would be tattling, or ratting someone out. But there are some important differences between tattling and telling. *Tattling* is when you're intentionally trying to get someone in trouble for doing something that doesn't even directly affect you or those you care about. An example of tattling would be telling a teacher that one of your classmates stayed out past his curfew last weekend. You just want that person to get busted. *Telling* is different. It involves informing an adult of a problem that directly affects the safety or well-being of you or a friend so that the adult can do something about it. You could also think of telling as *reporting*. You're reporting what you saw or experienced so that adults can get involved if necessary.

When trying to decide if you are tattling or reporting, ask yourself what you're trying to accomplish by sharing the information you have. If your real goal is to get somebody in trouble, especially for doing something that's harmless, then it might be tattling. If, on the other hand, you're trying to stop the other person from doing something that would hurt you or someone else, then it's reporting—and the right thing to do.

Snap a Screenshot

Never taken a screenshot before? Give it a try now! Most computer keyboards have a "Print Screen" or "PrtScn" key that will copy whatever is visible on your screen. Then you can paste the image into a word processing or photo editing file and save it. On Macs, you can take a screenshot by pressing the Command key, the Shift key, and the 3 key at the same time.

Cell phones and other mobile devices also let you easily take (and save) screenshots. For example, on Apple devices such as iPhones, you can press the "Home" and "Sleep" buttons at the same time. This will save a copy of the screen to the device's Camera Roll. Most new Android devices allow users to take screenshots by pressing the "Volume Down" and "Power" buttons at the same time. The image will then show up in your Gallery app. Older Android models may vary in the way to take a screenshot, though, so it's best to search online for instructions for your specific phone or tablet.

3. Never Retaliate

The fact that there is always evidence of cyberbullying means it's very important that you never retaliate against the person who cyberbullied you. This can be hard—*really* hard. You might want to get revenge for being hurt, or show that you aren't going to put up with being treated badly. Maybe your friends know what's going on and you don't want to look weak. You may be tempted to react angrily to make a point. And it's easy to do when you have a computer or cell phone at hand. But this will most likely backfire.

Think about it this way: If the cyberbullying gets really serious and you need to ask an adult for help, it's very important that all of the evidence clearly shows that the other person was bullying you. If you're responding with your own mean, hurtful, or inappropriate comments, though, it could look more like a disagreement or fight, and might not be considered bullying.

Or what if another person has been harassing you for months on end, and you just can't take it anymore? You might be so sick and tired of the situation that you finally crack under the pressure and post, text, or send something malicious about that person. What happens if he responds by reporting what you did? There's a good chance that *you* will get in trouble—even though you were the one being bullied in the first place! So even when you're really tempted to strike back, try your best not to. Be careful not to say anything online that an adult might interpret as bullying. Again, this can be hard. But it will be even harder to explain who's really at fault if you retaliate.

4. Talk About It

If you're being cyberbullied—or if you're dealing with any other issue in your life—it helps a lot to talk about how you feel and what's going on. Whether you choose to talk to a parent, teacher, coach, counselor, or friend, never keep the fact that you're being bullied to yourself. At first, you may think you can deal with the cyberbullying on your own. Or, you may not think anyone can truly help, and you figure talking won't solve the problem anyhow. Maybe you feel like you don't want to burden other people with your situation. However, being bullied—online or offline—can make it feel like you're trapped in a room where the walls are closing in. It can feel almost suffocating.

"Never be bullied into silence. Never allow yourself to be made a victim. Accept no one's definition of your life; define yourself."
—Harvey Fierstein